IRAN'S
Revolution

IRAN'S
Revolution

THE SEARCH FOR CONSENSUS

EDITED BY

R. K. RAMAZANI

Indiana University Press
Bloomington and Indianapolis

Published in association with
the Middle East Institute
Washington, DC

The following chapters appeared previously in *The Middle East Journal, Volume* 43 (No. 2, Spring 1989): Richard Cottam, "Inside Revolutionary Iran"; Shaul Bakhash, "The Politics of Land, Law, and Social Justice in Iran"; R. K. Ramazani, "Iran's Foreign Policy: Contending Orientations"; Anthony Parsons, "Iran and Western Europe"; and Gary Sick, "Trial by Error: Reflections on the Iran-Iraq War."

Manufactured in the United States of America

Library of Congress Cataloging-in-Publication Data

Iran's revolution: the search for consensus / edited by R.K. Ramazani.
    p.   cm.
    ISBN 0-253-34796-3.—ISBN 0-253-20548-4 (pbk.)
    1. Iran—Politics and government—1979–2. Iran—Foreign relations—1979-   I. Ramazani, Rouhollah K.
    DS318.825.17   1989
    320.955—dc20
                                                                89-7516
                                                                CIP

1   2   3   4   5   94   93   92   91   90

Contents

Preface

Iran has been a major player on the Middle Eastern stage since ancient times. Arnold Toynbee characterized it as the sole superpower of the ancient world; Iran's contributions to Islamic civilization and to the literary and cultural heritage of the world have indeed been substantial. Today, Iran is the largest Shi'i-inhabited country in the world and the only state ruled by an Islamic cleric. With the largest population and possibly the strongest industrial base of all the Gulf countries, Iran holds the second richest natural gas reserves in the world as well as important reserves of oil.

For the late Ayatollah Ruhollah Khomeini and his supporters, however, the single most important feature of Iran's uniqueness was and is its "Islamic Revolution." Of all the revolutions of modern times, Khomeini believed that Iran's alone was divinely inspired. The French and Russian revolutions, as he said on the occasion of the eighth anniversary of the revolution, were largely inspired by material considerations. Khomeini's claim would seem to be supported by Alexis de Tocqueville, who said more than a hundred years ago that the French Revolution was a "political revolution," even though it "like Islam poured forth its soldiers, its apostles and its martyrs over the face of the earth."

For scholars outside Iran, the revolution may be viewed differently and from a variety of perspectives, a few of which are reflected in this volume. From a political perspective, the revolution may well have been one of the greatest populist explosions in human history, as Richard Cottam suggests in his chapter. The scholarly community seems to be unanimous in the opinion that the revolution, at its inception, was indeed supported by what Ayatollah Ali Khamenei calls "all strata of the society."

In the area of socioeconomics, the revolution's pivotal claim has been that it speaks for the "powerless" or the "disinherited" of the whole world, not merely of Iran or even of the Muslim world. The ruling elite believes that the amelioration of living conditions of the powerless requires, above all, social justice. As Shaul Bakhash explains, attempts to improve the lot of the poor have raised complex and agonizing questions about private property rights, legislative authority, Islamic law, and the role of the *faqih*. Debates about these problems parallel various controversies over whether the government should control national and foreign trade or instead allow free trade, with almost unlimited elbow room for the private sector.

My chapter examines revolutionary Iran's foreign policy, arguing that its hallmarks are the dynamic coexistence and competition of vastly different orientations toward the international system. Given the fluidity of Iranian revolutionary politics, these orientations are adopted and abandoned with sensational rapidity by factions and individuals within and outside the ruling political elite. Because the revolution itself was triggered partly by the cumulative effects of alienation from the United States, it is no wonder that mutual antagonism continues to plague US-Iranian relations.

The revolution stirred anti-Western sentiments that seemed to challenge the European Community's longstanding commercial and financial relations with Iran. And yet except for the United States, the industrial democracies seemed to be coping with the Iranian revolution in their economic dealings and, until the February 1989 Salman Rushdie affair, even in diplomatic affairs. In this area, Anthony Parson's chapter discusses specifically Britain, France, West Germany, and Italy.

The revolution also prompted the Iraqi invasion of Iran. Gary Sick shows that the nearly eight years of armed conflict between Iran and Iraq made this the longest and bloodiest war of blunders in the modern history of the Middle East. The conflict also set a precedent in the annals of warfare by unleashing chemical weapons and missiles against civilian populations. It violated international moral and legal bans against chemical warfare and threatened the principle of freedom of navigation, especially in regard to the oil shipments of nonbelligerents.

Iran's relations with the superpowers was to be governed by the doctrine of "neither East nor West," but in practice revolutionary Iran seemed to challenge the West more than the East, as pointed out in the chapter by Shireen Hunter. The challenges to the West, however, were more ideological than commercial or financial; even the European-Iranian row over the Rushdie affair and the break in the newly established relations with Britain were not allowed to jeopardize Iranian economic ties with the West.

Furthermore, although the Iranian Revolution posed formidable challenges to US foreign policy, the revolutionary leaders managed over a turbulent decade to retain the option of eventually normalizing relations with the United States, as suggested in my chapter "Challenges for US Policy."

It had appeared for a while that the Islamic Republic of Iran was returning to a more normal political life, as evidenced by the encouragement of some freedom of expression. Khomeini had proclaimed that the absence of consensus on many controversial topics was no reason for him to cut off debate among factions. On the contrary, he believed that unhampered scholarly debate was the course most likely to lead Iran to its "ultimate best."

As one might have expected, however, that apparent promise of freedom of expression was intended for only those factions and individuals that held the absolute trust of the ruling theocratic elite. Under such circumstances, even the loyal opposition complained that some overzealous officials had targeted them for harassment and violence. The "counterrevolutionaries," on the other hand, charged human rights violations and, yet, sought to overthrow the incumbent regime by equally violent means. A United Nations report in November 1988 charged that in the previous months a "wave of executions" had been carried out against "members of various opposition groups" in Iran, including the Mujahidin-e Khalq. The forces of this group fought the Tehran government from bases in Iraq. Some observers surmised that the executions reflected a backlash of revenge against this particular dissident group, but others suspected of disloyalty to the government had also been executed.

Although Majlis Speaker Ali Akbar Hashemi-Rafsanjani did not mention such political realities, he frankly acknowledged that the Islamic Republic had not found satisfactory answers for other major social problems. On September 24, 1988, he told a group of clergymen at Qom:

> We still have not been able to clarify for people economic problems as befits Islam: We have differences of opinion among ourselves over these issues. We have not come forward with clear theses [principles] for our foreign policy. We have not evolved any new policies regarding social and cultural issues, minorities, and debatable religious matters (*mosthab*), which differ vastly from the early era of Islam to today, when we live under new conditions....

For the Iranian leaders, then, the real question is this: Why, by the end of the first decade of their revolution, have they failed to find solutions to so many problems? One can only speculate that the difficulty lies partly in one of the most ancient and tenacious tendencies in Iran's political culture—the adoption of unrealizable goals and inappropriate means. But it is not inevitable that this tendency should continue into the second decade of the Islamic Republic. The difficulty also lies in the kaleidoscopic variety of Iranian domestic and foreign policy during the Khomeini period. Iran's acceptance of the cease-fire in the war with Iraq appeared to mark the beginning of the return of its revolution to a degree of stable equilibrium. But the Rushdie affair seemed to turn back the hands of the clock. If the passing of Khomeini should result in a less ideological and more realistic approach to domestic and foreign policy, then one may hope that the revolution will finally enter what historian Crane Brinton calls "a state of 'normalcy.' "

With the ascendancy of Hashemi-Rafsanjani to the Presidency, this hope seemed justified. In his inaugural address to the Iranian Parliament on August 17, 1989, he said with characteristic frankness:

> This country has great potential for economic growth, but since we came to power, we have not done much [to achieve it].

Coping with widespread economic problems is the highest priority of the Rafsanjani administration. Its success or failure in achieving a better standard of living for the Iranian people is bound to have both domestic and international consequences.

No Iranian leader enjoys the same kind of religious and revolutionary legitimacy that characterized the leadership of the late Ayatollah Khomeini. Domestically, the new Iranian leaders will therefore have to combine successful performance in economic development with revolutionary credentials in order to command authority and maintain regime stability. In President Hashemi-Rafsanjani's words, "dams cannot be built by slogans [alone]."

Internationally, ideology must take serious note of reality if Iran's economic growth is to contribute to the resurgence of Iranian power in world politics. Despite unbridgeable ideological conflict with the Soviet Union, post-Khomeini Iran is forging unprecedented ties with Moscow partly as a means of aiding its economic development and post-war reconstruction. The international crisis that followed the Israeli abduction of Sheik Abdul Karim Obeid on July 28, 1989, the day Hashemi-Rafsanjani was elected president, suddenly revived the thorny issue of normalization of Iran's relations with the United States. Fortuitously, this crisis may eventually redound to Iran's advantage if it results in the resumption of economic relations between Tehran and Washington. American capital and technology can greatly expedite Iran's economic recovery, and Iran will be able to shape a more balanced strategic relationship with the superpowers.

R. K. Ramazani

IRAN'S
Revolution

Inside
Revolutionary Iran

Richard Cottam

The revolution of Iran was one of the greatest populist explosions in
human history. It marked the appearance of mass politics as a characteristic feature of Iran and was a portent of major change in the Third
World. Its implications for alterations in the world balance of power—
just one example of the change in interstate relations it forecasts—
have yet to be understood. Also at issue are important questions regarding the focus of political community identity, whether ethnic or
religious, and the persistence of Euro-American political culture as a
model for world emulation. At the moment of victory, the magnitude
of support for the revolution was apparent to any observer. As much
as one-fifth of the population had demonstrated on one day in December 1978 against a regime still capable of inflicting a heavy price on
the demonstrators, but within a year's time, the support for the new
revolutionary regime had shrunk dramatically to an intensely loyal
core base. That support base, though clearly a minority, provided the
regime with the strength to stand against internal attacks by elements
that had eliminated much of its top leadership and against a major
external challenge from Iraq and its Arab allies and to some degree
from both superpowers and much of Europe. This article presents a
description and explanation of the failures and successes, both with
dramatic dimensions, of the regime's first decade.[1]

The Revolutionary Leadership

The most conspicuous and important feature of the Iranian revolu-

3

tion was the polarization process that quickly developed. Following victory, the revolution in short order eliminated Iran's sociopolitical elite from the center stage. Much of the revolution's leadership came from that elite, including Mehdi Bazargan, the most prominent of the revolutionary leaders inside Iran and the first prime minister of the Islamic Republic of Iran. Within one year, almost all of the revolutionary leaders who could be considered part of the old elite had been pushed outside the revolution.

From the beginning of the revolution, there was power asymmetry among the revolutionary leadership. Inside Iran, most of the leaders had been associated with the regime of former Prime Minister Muhammad Mossadegh or viewed the revolution as a continuation of Mossadegh's movement.[2] Within this group were the secular National Front and the religious liberal Freedom Front, which counted among its members many revolutionary clerics. In addition, a leftist leadership, both secular and religious, played a major role in the revolutionary process but not in the central revolutionary leadership. The revolution, however, had a charismatic leader in the person of Ayatollah Ruhollah Khomeini, and early on it was apparent that the breadth of his popularity among large sections of the public gave him an influence potential that dwarfed all others. Khomeini had the ability to define the revolution, and the more perceptive of the other revolutionary leaders understood this well. In the months just before the revolution, these leaders searched for a formula that would provide them with some control of revolutionary dynamics. They designed various transitional schemes for this purpose, but each such scheme called for the cooperation of the shah and the US government.[3] Once it was apparent that no such cooperation would be forthcoming, their only real hope was that Khomeini could be maneuvered into playing the role of the legitimizing agent, rather than the directing agent, of the revolutionary regime.

The weakness of the liberal leadership was most apparent when viewed in terms of the organizational base of the revolution. The National Front and the Freedom Front were essentially elite organizations with scant ability to establish a mass base of support, but the leftist factions, secular and religious, did have disciplined organizations capable of reaching sections of the educated youth. They were better adapted to the clandestine political and paramilitary activities than to mobilizing the large sectors of the population that were increasingly predisposed to revolutionary activity. It was the mosque that served the purpose of reaching and giving political direction to this rapidly growing base and the mosque bureaucracy that provided the organizational discipline. When the revolution succeeded and governmental institutions collapsed with a totality usually associated with a catastrophic military defeat, these mosque-based organizations served the purpose of maintaining order, providing basic services, and defending the new revolutionary regime.

Polarization

The polarization process began almost immediately with the revolutionary victory. The liberal leadership had called for the rule of law, the return of basic freedoms, respect for the dignity of the individual, and a concern for social justice. The new revolutionary organizations—self-appointed courts, revolutionary committees established in all sections of the cities, and roving groups of youths determined to exact "revolutionary justice"—began to act, however, in an arbitrary manner that belied the liberal goals the leaders had enunciated. Khomeini did appoint Bazargan, a man with the strongest of liberal credentials, as prime minister of the new provisional government, and Bazargan quickly selected a cabinet of religious and secular liberals who had the competence to administer the various ministries. These formal institutions were in great disarray and, until reorganization plans could be worked out, the revolutionary institutions operated as a surrogate government. Their behavior hardly conformed to the norms of liberal democracy. Executions following perfunctory trials became the focus of the international media's attention, and the Bazargan government, which could do little more than protest, appeared helpless, weak, and ineffectual.[4]

In the months that followed, the battle for control of the revolution would be fought in the context of a struggle for control of the revolutionary institutions. Bazargan's strategy was straightforward: As rapidly as the ministries could be reconstructed with new personnel and new directions, their jurisdiction should be restored; the revolutionary institutions could then be absorbed into the relevant ministries. To accomplish his strategic objectives, Bazargan required the cooperation of Khomeini and a steadily strengthening personal power base. Each revolutionary institution, however, quickly developed a vested interest in its own survival. An assertive, radically revolutionary clerical elite began to emerge within the leadership of these institutions and soon was fully capable of challenging the established leaders, both secular and religious.

Bazargan was able on occasion to prevail upon Khomeini to issue calls for unity and to agree that the governmental ministries should be able to reassert their jurisdictional rights. Despite these successes, the challenging elite also had access to Khomeini and succeeded frequently in delaying or reversing these decisions. Bazargan's primary failure, however, was his inability to construct a personal base of support. His natural support base was the educated middle class which by and large had accommodated the shah's regime and had joined the revolution only in the last months before its success. To mobilize this group in support of the government, Bazargan and his allies needed to transform the National Front and the Freedom Front into a major political organization. Even under the best of circumstances, such a task would have been difficult to carry out in a short period of time and, in Bazargan's case, this proved impossibly difficult for at least three reasons.

First, the actions of the revolutionary institutions, particularly the courts and the committees, appalled and frightened potential Bazargan supporters. Many took the first opportunity to leave the country and others moved toward full opposition to the regime. They described Bazargan as the Kerensky of the Iranian Revolution. In so doing they denied the formal government the leverage that only a strong base of support could provide. Second, Bazargan felt very much constrained by the necessity to convince Khomeini of his government's sincere support. Any strong alliance with secular elements or formation of a political party that appeared to be in the Western cultural mold could destroy Khomeini's trust in Bazargan.[5] Third, Bazargan's proven abilities as an underground leader were not well suited for his new role as leader of the government. To be sure, his task was a remarkably difficult one: to satisfy simultaneously a middle class that tended to be anti-clerical—and had yet to comprehend the importance of the appearance of a politically assertive mass that looked to religious leaders for guidance—and a charismatic leader who viewed secularism as a despicable cultural import from the imperial West. Given the circumstances, Bazargan's strategy was difficult to fault, but the tactical execution was often indecisive and inconsistent.

The Left, as a whole, underestimated the strength of a populist movement increasingly under clerical control. In the critical first months of Bazargan's premiership, they tacitly cooperated with the radical clerics in weakening and ultimately eliminating the liberal leadership that they saw as bourgeois and ultimately pro-American. The taking of American diplomats as hostages—an act that marked the end of the aspirations of liberals—received the enthusiastic support of the Left. With the liberals' defeat, the Left's weaknesses became all too apparent. At that point the Left split sharply in terms of preferred strategy. One section, consisting of the Mujahidin and a "minority" of the secular Fedayan, moved into increasingly violent opposition. The other section, consisting of the "majority" Fedayan and the Tudeh Party, cooperated with the regime hoping thereby to retain their ties with the newly assertive mass and possibly to offer themselves to that mass as an alternative leadership in the future. The Mujahidin carried out assassinations and bombing attacks on government leaders with dramatic success. The government responded with an 18-month reign of terror, and the opposition leftists were driven underground.[6] Having accomplished this, the regime in 1983 turned on the cooperating secular leftists and eliminated them as a significant political force.[7] At that point, the people of Iran were sharply polarized, but the pro-Khomeini pole was sufficiently strong to grant an essential stability to the regime.

Khomeini's Command

The charismatic appeal of Ayatollah Khomeini proved to be both persistent and intense for a significant element, albeit surely a minority, of the Iranian population. His appeal was the primary basis of control on which the authority of the Islamic Republic rested and gave Khomeini the ability to define his regime. The official position he occupied, that of vice regent, the *faqih* of the *vilayet-e faqih*, was possibly granted the greatest latitude for making critical decisions of any constitutionally ordained position in constitutional history. Despite this, from the outset he indicated that his function would be that of a guide, one who because of his profound understanding of the model of a just government inherent in the Quran and the *sharia* would be in a position to guide his government along the correct path. To a large degree, this interpretation prevailed in practice. When Khomeini made a firm decision, such as to keep the American diplomats hostage or to persist in a devastating war with Iraq, his decision was accepted as absolutely binding on his government regardless of any deep reservations his officials may have held. Far more frequently, however, and sometimes concerning questions of vital concern, Khomeini may not only have failed to make a firm decision but may also have vacillated in his support of a decision made by his government. The result in matters of great domestic import was often one of policy paralysis.

In a situation such as this, in which an individual with dictatorial powers fails to furnish strategic direction for his government's policy, a reasonable expectation would be that someone within the government would begin to exercise powers in the name of the leader. The great anomaly of the Iranian situation is that this did not occur. The Iranian regime was authoritarian but lacked an individual or collective dictator. Khomeini did not permit any individual or faction to gain preeminence within his government. A persistent pattern of his leadership was to intervene in favor of leaders, or factions, who were loyal to the regime and who appeared to be losing in a struggle for control of the regime. Even in the case of Bazargan and Abol Hasan Bani-Sadr, whose reservations made their acceptance of the regime problematic, Khomeini appeared reluctant to accept the political demise of either.

Those Iranians who despised Khomeini tended to explain this behavior in devil theory terms—a malevolently brilliant leader who manipulates his supporters in a master strategy designed to negate any developing leader or group with the potential of challenging his position.[8] Others were inclined to see a leader who was unconcerned with the detail of policy and who placed an exceptionally high value on the unity of the faithful, regardless of the differences among them. Whatever the explanation, the consequences were clear enough.

Centralization of control, the preoccupation of Bazargan in the first months following the revolution, has yet to be achieved. Khomeini's unwillingness either to exercise close direction of policy or to permit any of his lieutenants to exercise that direction for him had an important consequence in terms of factional development.[9] The failure to give close direction to policy resulted in the appearance of a broad expression of policy preferences. Newspapers and magazines developed ideological personalities, and articles of a highly critical nature regarding matters of central policy were published. The range in economic positions held by leading members of the regime was particularly broad with advocates of both state control and of a laissez-faire doctrine finding forums. Disagreements over basic questions regarding the distribution of wealth divided regime supporters, even though Khomeini had taken strong but essentially abstract positions on social justice for the relatively deprived. Divisions also occurred over the extent of freedom considered acceptable. Advocacy of greater freedom of expression could be heard even from Khomeini's designated successor, Ayatollah Hoseyn Ali Montazeri.[10]

Possibly the most important division of opinion occurred over questions relating to the degree of requisite militancy regarding an ideological messianic purpose. All agreed that the revolution deserved to be exported, but for some this meant nothing more than creating a model Islamic regime that could be emulated; no major voice called for exporting the revolution through the force of arms. There was, however, a clear difference in receptivity to requests from non-Iranian leaders for material, diplomatic, and even clandestine military support to advance the revolution elsewhere. In the domain of foreign policy strategy, as elsewhere, the lack of central direction was apparent. Individual ambassadors and other officials felt free on many occasions to act in the name of Iran and often could generate some institutional support for their endeavors.[11] Uncertainty regarding Iran's actual policy inevitably followed.

Parliamentary elections and parliamentary behavior followed the same pattern.[12] Would-be candidates for election had to be approved by the Council of Guardians, and those approved clearly had to be supporters of the Islamic Republic regime. Among those who were accepted for candidacy, however, there was a broad ideological range and genuine competition. Voters had a choice in some issues of real consequence. Questions such as support for the regime or for a continuation of the war with Iraq could not be raised, however, and, in general, the campaigning did not focus sharply on political ideological differences. Within parliament, debates occurred although they were only rarely of qualitative distinction.

It is possible, however, to infer where individual deputies stood on a conservative-progressive scale and on particular issues. Factional attachments could also be inferred although with less confidence given the fluidity of the factions. The best indication of factional association was the position taken by deputies in confirmation hearings for nominees for cabinet positions. The rejection of governmental nominees who seemed to have at least the tacit approval of Ayatollah Khomeini was one of the most anomalous features of this most untypical of authoritarian regimes.[13]

The situation as described above was not conducive to the formation of cohesive factions. Khomeini's pattern of not permitting a faction to triumph can be illustrated by several decisions. In December 1987 and January 1988, Khomeini made several statements that could reasonably be interpreted as moving him in the direction of those who called for a strong governmental role in social reform and greater equality in income distribution.[14] The conservative-dominated Council of Guardians, which had negated many reformist measures, was rebuked and its veto position weakened. Khomeini also appeared to be criticizing the centrist president of the Islamic Republic, Ali Khamanei. The response, a public affirmation of Khomeini's infallible wisdom by all his lieutenants, was an effective reminder that the Iranian regime, despite the anomalies recounted above, was indeed authoritarian.

The position of the progressives remained strong through the spring election for the Majlis. Minister of Interior Hujjat al-Islam Ali Akbar Mohtashemi, considered by many the strong man of the progressive-radicals, presided over an election that saw the defeat of several influential conservatives.[15] Then, as Iran's military position deteriorated, Khomeini was prevailed upon and agreed to place Hujjat al-Islam Ali Akbar Hashemi-Rafsanjani, speaker of the Majlis, as the acting commander in chief of all the armed forces.[16] Hashemi-Rafsanjani, a man whose pragmatism inclined him toward taking positions compatible with conservative preferences, was able to move the center of power back again to the conservative side. When Prime Minister Mir Hoseyn Musavi, who was closer to the progressive end of the scale, sent his nominees for the cabinet to the Majlis, those most closely associated with Mohtashemi generally received the lowest votes, even though presumably the election had improved their positions, and several were rejected.[17] The high point of the conservative domination came with the approval of United Nations Resolution 598 and the acceptance of a cease-fire. Thereafter Khomeini refused to endorse either side and instead called for a free debate between them.

A Polarized Society

Iran, at the end of a decade of rule by the forces of the Islamic revolution, is deeply polarized. At one end of the scale a core support group has a persistingly intense attachment to the revolutionary regime. At the other end of the scale, a large group intransigently opposes the regime. The two groups know very little of each other; in fact, each tends to question the existence of the other as a significant element of the population. Then, in between the two, is what is surely a majority of Iranians who can be described as accommodators. They have little affection for the regime, but see little likelihood of its passing from the scene any time soon. Whereas the intransigently opposed have left Iran in large numbers, the accommodators have remained and have adapted the routine of their lives to the cultural and political demands of the regime. In many cases they have prospered and in most cases are not intolerably uncomfortable. It is of course impossible to estimate the relative sizes of the three groups with any confidence, but the evidence is that each is significantly large. So, too, is evidence of the attitudes that characterize each group.

Government Supporters

The most telling evidence of the size and importance of the core support group is evidenced by the crisis behavior of the regime. The regime easily survived assassinations and bombings carried out by the Mujahidin that decimated its top leadership. That type of resilience must reflect a popular support base from which new leaders can be drawn and which grants the regime unwavering support in moments of extreme duress. Similarly, the response to the Iraqi invasion in September 1980 reflected a willingness to risk making the ultimate sacrifice for the defense of the regime and the religio-national community on which it was based. The Iranian performance was clearly a surprise to Saddam Hussein and other Iraqi officials. Their statements at the time of the attack reflected an expectation of a quick collapse of the Khomeini regime.[18] The eight-year war was fought largely by young men recruited from the core support group. Their willingness to stand against an enemy who controlled the air and was equipped with greatly superior weaponry is legendary. Iran was badly mauled the last year of the war, but the point should not be overlooked that it was standing alone against an enemy equipped and supported by much of the world. Equally persuasive is the evidence given above of the willingness of the regime to grant those who supported the regime a large degree of freedom. Such behavior reflects the regime's confidence that it is fully legitimate for this element of the population.

The composition of the large assemblies of people who attend the Friday prayers and the pro-government demonstrations indicates, as does the recruitment base for the Revolutionary Guard Corps, the nature of the social support base of the regime. Deeply religious, it consists of individuals who have turned to their religious leaders for personal guidance throughout their lives. Supporters of the regime are from urban lower and lower-middle classes, Persian- or Turki-speaking, and adherents of Shi'i Islam. The lack of success of Iraq's appeal to Arabic-speaking citizens of Iran, especially the Shia, suggests that support from this community is also substantial. There were clear manifestations before the Iraqi attack, however, of dissatisfaction in that community. There has been little evidence that the regime has succeeded in attracting strong support from the Sunni community, and strong anti-regime movements have appeared in the Kurdish, Turkman, and Baluchi ethnic communities which are predominantly Sunni.[19]

The ability of the regime to attract sustained and intense support from lower and lower-middle class elements is one of the major indications of the breadth and depth of change that has occurred in Iran. At the time of Mossadegh, this element of the population was largely unconcerned with political affairs and unaffected by Mossadegh's charismatic appeal, which was very strong within the middle and upper-middle class. Traditional politicians in the Mossadegh era who used mercenary crowds for their demonstrations would purchase the participation of their demonstrators from precisely this element of the population. Likewise, religio-political leaders, such as Ayatollah Abol Qasem Kashani, would transport thousands of such people to their demonstrations, but at the time there was little indication of any sustained political commitment among these demonstrators. Most ironic of all, the largely mercenary mobs, purchased with CIA money, that marched from south Tehran against Mossadegh on August 19, 1953 and were the critical factor in his overthrow, were drawn precisely from the group that in this decade has been the most loyal supporter of the Islamic regime.[20]

The Iranian regime under Khomeini was a unique manifestation of authoritarian populism. As with other regimes of this variety, including European fascism, a characteristic and probably essential ingredient of success is the presence of a charismatic leader. Such a leader attracts unquestioning support from a substantial mass base primarily by an ability to manipulate symbols that have a natural and intense appeal. One such set of symbols is that which relates to a political community to which the people feel an intense identity. Most commonly that community is ethnic and the symbols are national symbols. For Khomeini, the community was the Islamic *'ummah*. Khomeini tried to avoid limiting the symbolic appeal of his movement to the sectarian Shi'i component of the 'ummah, but his success in this endeavor was limited. As the Iran-Iraq conflict continued, seemingly without prospect of an end, his ability to appeal symbolically to intensely religious Sunni Arabs waned.[21]

The embodiment of the symbolic appeal of the Iranian regime was in the form of its leader, Ayatollah Khomeini, the imam of the 'ummah. Khomeini was the guide who showed the way to submission to God, to the good society where the deprived could receive succor and self-realization, to the path by which the oppressed could gain the courage to stand up to the oppressors, and to the unity of the community of believers. Herein also lay a major weakness of regime control. Its primary means of control lay with the charismatic appeal of a mortal, aging, and ailing leader. No subordinate leader developed an appeal that even remotely approached that of Khomeini, including his one-time designated successor, Ayatollah Montazeri. At the very least, with Khomeini's passing from the scene, the regime must strengthen other modes of control and, in the short term, that probably means the coercive arm.

The regime's control over its support base through a system of benefits should not be underestimated, however. That section of the Iranian population, much of which has come alive politically only in the last 15 years, has seen the distribution of societal reward shifted in its favor. Its political influence is at an unimagined level, and official concern for its material well-being has never been greater. To be sure, the economy of Iran has suffered, especially as a consequence of the war but, in relative terms, those who most support the regime see their position as improving. With the passing of Khomeini, however, there will surely be a greater insistence on improvements in the material well-being of this now fully awakened mass.

This mass support base is the key to regime stability and hence the source of real strength for the regime, but the same cannot be said for the new governing elite. The coming to power of an authoritarian populist regime is almost always at the expense of much of the old sociopolitical elite. This was certainly the case in Iran as the revolution evolved into its authoritarian populist form. Of the old sociopolitical elite, only a section of its clerical component remains. In its place is a new elite composed of clerics and highly religious laymen. A thin elite, it has yet to achieve broad acceptance. Some impressive figures have appeared within it, but by and large it is still of limited competence. Furthermore, the regime is having considerable difficulty recruiting a technocratically competent intelligentsia into its ranks. University students and professionals who must staff the bureaucracy appear to be better classified as a group among the accommodators than among the regime supporters.[22]

The Opposition

Evidence of the size and significance of the intransigent opposition is much more obvious to the outside observer. It exists in the form of the hundreds of thousands of Iranians who have left their country and who are highly articulate in giving expression to their hatred for the regime. It exists as well in the willingness of leaders from this group to ally with mortal enemies of the Iranian regime. The fact that the most militant and effective of opposition groups, the Mujahidin, would ally with Saddam Hussein and fully cooperate with him in his attacks on Iran tells a great deal about the intensity of the hatred for the Khomeini government. Other leaders, such as Shapour Bakhtiar, who opposed the shah as a puppet of the United States and Israel, turned precisely to the United States and Israel to solicit support for the overturn of this regime.

The opposition includes many whose values embrace secularism and who are attracted to the social and cultural norms of the West. Khomeini viewed them as acculturated—pathetic imitators of an alien society. Inevitably, the primary mode of control of this section of the population is coercion. Optimal success exists when the coerced element sees no real possibility of overturning the regime. In authoritarian populism, the primary source of coercion is not to be found in terror instruments, such as SAVAK, but rather in the realization that the regime is supported intensely by a section of the population fully willing and able to defend it internally including brutalizing those who are in opposition. This is the case in the Islamic Republic regime. The local committees, the Revolutionary Guard, and youths described as *hizballahi* are seen as fearsome enforcers. Terror in Iran today, as compared with the days of the shah, is essentially decentralized. Its unpredictability is one of its most frightening features for its targets.

The intransigent opposition tends not to think seriously of joining the factional struggle within Iran. As described above, this was for a time the strategy of a major section of the secular Left, including the Tudeh and the "majority" Fedayan. Following the suppression of these groups in 1983, they dropped this strategy and called instead for a united front strategy of at least the Center and Left.

The leaders of royalist and secular nationalist opinion operate outside Iran. Their strategic efforts follow two directions. Like the secular Left, they call for a united front of the opposition and hope to use the large exile community as a base for future activities inside Iran. The real focus of their activity, however, has been to persuade external forces, and this means particularly the US government, to return them to power inside Iran. Overwhelmingly, they believe that Khomeini's success was a consequence of American machinations.[23] Totally convinced of US omnipotence, they concentrate on convincing Washington of the terrible mistake it made by allowing or manipulating the success of the revolution. The rationale they attribute to the Americans is that Khomeini, anti-communist and enormously popular, was a preferred ally for the US strategy of containing communist expansion. Their arguments, therefore, are that Khomeini was either an instrument of communist expansion—a typical royalist line—or that he was creating a political environment in Iran that was susceptible to Soviet subversion. Their suggestions for the ideal US response involve generating a coup, much like that of 1953 and, in addition, providing the means and support for a military movement into Iran by exile military forces. Efforts to solicit external support have generally failed. Turkey and Pakistan have established good relations with Iran and appear to have turned a deaf ear to the Iranian opposition's entreaties. Financial support has come from Iraq and probably from Saudi Arabia, but only Iraq has been willing to offer major assistance to opposition activities.

There is little reason to doubt that all of the opposition groups have important contacts and organized activities inside Iran, but the only organizations with proven major assets inside the country are the Kurdish Democratic Party headed by Abdul Rahman Qassemlu and the Mujahidin headed by Massoud Rajavi. Former President Bani-Sadr maintains an organization with important contacts especially among religious circles inside Iran. The three men for a time coordinated their activities and constituted the one force with some potential for political and paramilitary maneuvering inside the country.[24] Their alliance broke up, however, and both Qassemlu and Rajavi moved to take advantage of the Iran-Iraq conflict to enlist significant Iraqi support. The cease-fire negotiations and Saddam Hussein's use of chemical weapons against Iraqi Kurds have destroyed any likelihood of a major Iraqi contribution to the Kurds' future efforts. The Mujahidin clearly have a clandestine organization capable of inflicting damage inside Iran, but their appeal internally appears to be small.

The one focus of opposition to the regime that continues to operate inside Iran is the liberal remnant of the original revolutionary leadership. Mehdi Bazargan continues to write, speak, and engage in dialogue with both regime supporters and opponents in Tehran. He is the one Iranian leader inside the country who enjoys a genuinely independent popularity, i.e., one not derived from his association with Khomeini. His one-time foreign minister, Ibrahim Yazdi, is also continuing efforts to refocus the regime on what he sees as its original values and purposes. They work within a community of like-minded individuals whose backgrounds are with the National Front, the Freedom Front, and the Radical Movement of Iran. They include individuals with the deepest of religious convictions and others who are devotedly secular. Their position is, of course, tenuous at best. Yet the tolerance they receive from the regime, despite the omnipresent threat of suppression and persecution, is an indication of a continued devotion to freedom of expression among some of the regime leadership. The hope that the regime might initiate its own policy of *glasnost* is not completely without foundation.

The Accommodating Majority

Evidence of the existence of the large group of accommodators, adapting to but granting the regime little or no real support, is strong but more subtle. It is seen most obviously in the willingness of these Iranians to complain openly to strangers on the streets, buses, or in taxis about the quality of life and the quality of the government. Given the arbitrariness of the application of terror, this open criticism involves some risk, but the complaints are much too widespread to elicit that kind of response except when there is suspicion of a direct connection to a group such as the Mujahidin. Evidence is also seen in the lack of interest in elections in which there is a degree of genuine choice. The accommodators are likely to vote because they fear possible punishment for not voting. They tend, however, to see any candidate who is a regime supporter, as all are, as one with whom they cannot relate even though they may much prefer the actual policies of either the conservatives or progressives. Earlier in the history of elections in the Islamic Republic, it was possible to infer whom among the candidates the accommodators found least unappealing. In the election of 1988, however, there was little indication of such a pattern.[25]

Possibly the best evidence of the accommodationist attitude toward the regime appeared at the time of the Iraqi missile attacks on Tehran and other Iranian cities. We have come to expect that bombings of this nature are counterproductive as devices for destroying civilian morale, even when they inflict substantial but not really devastating damage. The bombings tend to harden the civilians' hatred and their willingness to fight back against their tormentors. In the Iranian case, there was little evidence of this kind of a response. The middle class, especially, fled the cities, manifesting an attitude of fleeing a war in which they had no real stake and for which they had no interest in making any personal sacrifice. Dislike of Iraq may have been intense, but it was paralleled by a dislike of an Iranian government with which they could not relate and which they saw as lacking any real legitimacy.[26]

The accommodators see little that would lead them to believe that the regime is seriously vulnerable to being overthrown. There is, in other words, a low sense of political efficacy within this majority. Like the intransigent oppositionists, they tend to believe that the Islamic revolution as it evolved was a direct product of external machinations, particularly from the CIA. Unable to leave the country, or preferring to remain there, they are willing to adapt to an unhappy situation and to make the most of their lives. They would be responsive, it follows, to a governmental utilitarian strategy—one that results in an improved economy and opportunities for a satisfactory career. They would view with deep distaste any foreign adventure and have little interest in a foreign policy that uses Iranian resources in the interests of "oppressed" foreigners, such as the Palestinians.

Conclusion

At the close of World War II, the focus of populist appeal in Iran, as in the Arab world, was on secular nationalist leaders such as Mossadegh. Even then, nationalist leaders had to recognize the great popular attraction of Islamic leaders. In the process of mobilizing support for regimes, such as Mossadegh's, which were seeking to assert real independence for their people, a coalition with Islamic leaders was highly beneficial. In the Cold War era, the nationalist leadership of Iran was defeated and discredited in large part because of external intervention and, as a consequence of that defeat, lost the center stage of populist appeal. By the early 1960s, Ayatollah Khomeini was emerging as the great populist leader for the next generation and the individual most capable of mobilizing the Iranian people for the effort to regain control of their own destiny.

Khomeini aspired to give those he described as oppressed peoples an example in Iran of an oppressed people standing up to the great oppressors. He aspired as well to provide an example of a government

that succeeded in bringing to Iran "the just society." When his lieutenants persuaded him to accept Resolution 598, however, they did so
with the accompanying admission that they had, at least temporarily,
failed in achieving these great tasks. Iran, they admitted, was being
portrayed successfully, especially in the Arab world, as an aggressor
willing to resort to terrorism, as concerned only with the Shi'i sect,
and as anything but an example of the just society.[27] They pointed to
the Palestinian uprising, the success of Islam in Egypt and North Africa, and to the continued oppression from the oppressors and their
lackeys as indicative both of the opportunity and the need for a revital-
ization of the Iranian example.[28]

The balance sheet for revolutionary Iran must include both these
elements. The regime has indeed demonstrated its ability to withstand
great challenges, both internal and external. In the process, it should
have demonstrated to its own people and to the world that the power
calculations of the previous era must be altered sharply. With the appearance of mass politics in the Third World, the conclusion is apparent that the era of easy interventionism in the Third World by supposedly Great Powers has come to an end. Middle powers such as Iran
must be considered far more seriously in terms of capability than has
been the case in the past. Yet, these conclusions are not being drawn
either at home or in the world at large. As described above, much,
possibly most, of the Iranian population persists in regarding the
Khomeini regime as having been foreign-imposed, and US and European involvement in the Persian Gulf reflect a persisting Euro-
American refusal to recognize the shift in the balance of power implied
by Iran's ability to stand alone against much of the world.

On the other hand, the dashing of Khomeini's messianic hopes was
not simply the consequence of a propaganda defeat, as his lieutenants
seemed to suggest. The decline in the early appeal of Khomeini to others in the Middle East and Third World was due in part to the underes-
timation of the persisting importance of ethnic community and sectarian identity. Regardless of Khomeini's eloquent claims to represent the
broader Islamic 'ummah and to speak for the world's oppressed, his
regime was perceived as being driven by Iranian and/or Shi'i objectives. Arabs, including those favoring Islamic governments, who be-

lieved initially that the Iraqi attack on Iran was a mistake of historic proportion, gradually came to see the Iran-Iraq conflict as one in which they had no choice but to side with their Arab brothers.[29]

Internal Iranian political developments have also proven difficult to reconcile with the just society model. The early executions, the failure to restore to Iran the rule of law, the polarization of the population, and the willingness to acquiesce in the brutalization of those who opposed clerical rule seemed a far cry from an ideal model.[30] Regime leaders are proclaiming their determination to reconstruct Iran and, in so doing, to restore the early lost promise. Their task will be exceedingly difficult. Furthermore, the leadership is deeply divided over the strategy for achieving this end. The specific issue of concern is the extent to which Iran should interact with the outside world, including that sector described as the oppressors, in the process of reconstruction. One major tendency, represented by Hashemi-Rafsanjani and, to a lesser extent, by Khamenei, calls for an entirely pragmatic approach. When foreign experts and foreign contractors can provide services not to be found in Iran, they should be utilized. The effort to attract technocratically competent exiles should also be pursued vigorously.[31] Presumably those advocating this policy are prepared to pay the costs for it. That would involve at least a major effort to normalize diplomatic relations with many states castigated as part of the oppressor world and to avoid the appearance and the substance of aiding groups that engage in acts of terrorism. It would involve as well internal relaxation both of institutionally-based and mob coercion. An exercise of greater centralization of control would be essential as would also a downgrading of redistributional policies.

The other strategic tendency, represented by Prime Minister Musavi, Interior Minister Mohtashemi, and Prosecutor General Muhammad Asqar Musavi Khoiniha is far more ideological. The call is for reconstruction to be in the hands of committed Iranians with little reliance on foreign experts and contractors.[32] They argue that anything less would risk the loss of direction of the Islamic revolution. They are adamantly opposed to any significant rapprochement with the United States, and they tend to draw a major distinction between the evil purposes of the United States and the Soviet Union. They wish to follow a policy of aiding revolutionary forces and presumably would look with favor upon solicitations of aid from elements within the Arab world who advocate Islamic revolutions in their countries. Khomeini's pronouncements on these matters of contention were inconclusive.[33] The issue therefore stands as one around which factional conflict is likely to crystallize.

A second major issue is one that has prevailed throughout the past decade: the direction of institutional development. Should the revolutionary institutions be brought under, and indeed incorporated within, traditional government ministries? What institutions have the regime developed that could serve the purpose of recruiting individuals into the new governing elite, preferably individuals with the technical competence to staff critical bureaucratic positions in the organizational base of the regime? What institutions would serve to explain and attract support for the policies of the regime? In many authoritarian systems this function is performed by an official authoritarian single party, and there were early indications that the Islamic Republic Party would serve this purpose for Iran. The dissolution of that party in 1987 is, however, indicative of the evolution of the disagreement concerning the proper institutional base for the regime. The Islamic Republic Party served well the function of rallying supporters of clerical rule in Iran, but once Bazargan, and later Bani-Sadr, was defeated, clerical rule was an established fact; the party became little more than a reflection of the ebb and flow of factional formations and dissolutions. As such, it mirrored Khomeini's apparent preference that no faction prevail and served more to underline existing dissensus than to recruit and prepare a new generation for leadership in the regime. Because it served no useful purpose it was dissolved.[34]

Responding to a clear need to give the regime a strong and dedicated institutional base, ambitious and dedicated individuals began to transform some of the revolutionary institutions to serve this purpose. Foremost among these was the Revolutionary Guard. It evolved from the pro-regime youth groups that seized control of the streets in the final days of the old regime and served the critical function of a coercive force providing stability and order for the new regime. After that, the Revolutionary Guard developed into an institution that was capable of fighting the invading Iraqi army to a standstill, played a major role in maintaining internal order, and gave protection to government officials. Its role expanded into clandestine internal and external operations designed to safeguard the revolutionary regime at home and to give support to non-Iranians who asked for assistance to put pressure on or to overturn external regimes. In sum, the Revolutionary Guard began to absorb the functions of the military services, the police, an internal security organization, an intelligence agency with operations at home and abroad, and even of the foreign policy departments. Together with other institutions, such as the Reconstruction Jihad—an organization dedicated to developing and executing programs that would improve the economic and social situation of deprived, and especially rural, sections of the population—and the Office of Islamic Guidance, the revolutionary institutions began to develop into an institutional underlay essential for long-term stability and legitimacy. More traditional institutions, such as the Ministry of Justice, were able to adapt fairly easily to the abstract model of a "just government," and still others, such as Heavy Industry, were led by individuals who were dedicated to the task of translating an ambiguous and abstract Islamic ideology programmatically.

When Khomeini issued instructions that called for a strong and assertive government, his words were interpreted as giving support to those who were attempting to establish these institutional bases. For several months, including the period of new parliamentary elections, the more revolutionary-minded of Iranian leaders appeared to be operating with the sanction of the imam of the 'ummah. As the Iranian military situation began to deteriorate in 1988 and, in response, Khomeini assigned Hashemi-Rafsanjani the task of bringing unity to the armed forces, there was a shift back again to the more conservative side of the factional struggle. At issue was the vitality of the very institutional base that served particularly well the purpose of the more revolutionary-minded. Rumors of downgrading Revolutionary Guard commanders were widespread. The familiar pattern of Khomeini's leadership was continuing.

At the close of the Islamic Republic's first decade, the prognosis is mixed. Much of its strength was the direct product of Khomeini's charismatic appeal. With his passing, major adjustments must be made. Should the more conservative of his lieutenants prevail, those adjustments might well lead to a broadened but far less enthusiastic base of support. Should the more radical of his lieutenants prevail, the loss of Khomeini's charismatic appeal as a means of maintaining support could only be compensated for in the short-run by a much greater reliance on the coercive instruments of control. The polarization of the Iranian society, a product of Khomeini's leadership style, is the primary source of regime vulnerability. The two ideological orientations being advanced suggest vastly different approaches for dealing with that problem. Khomeini gave a personal definition to the first decade of the regime; the next decade is likely to produce a major redefinition.

NOTES

1. For a full description of the rhythmic change in revolutionary Iran see Shaul Bakhash, *The Reign of the Ayatollahs: Iran and the Islamic Revolution* (New York: Basic Books, 1984) and Dilip Hiro, *Iran Under the Ayatollahs* (Boston: Routledge and Kegan Paul, 1985).
2. Bazargan has described the leadership composition in some detail. See Mehdi Bazargan, *Shurai Enqelab va Dolat Movaqat* (The Revolutionary Council and the Provisional Government) (Tehran: Sandoq Pesati, 1984), pp. 35-40.
3. For a description of the transitional scheme rationale see Richard Cottam, *Iran and the United States: A Cold War Case Study* (Pittsburgh: The University of Pittsburgh Press, 1988), chapter 5.
4. See Oriana Fallaci, "Everybody Wants to Boss," *New York Times Magazine*, October 28, 1979.
5. Bazargan describes Khomeini's views in *Shurai Enqelab va Dolat Movaqat*, pp. 18-44. See also Mehdi Bazargan, *Enqelab-e Iran dar Dau Harekat* (The Iranian Revolution in Two Phases) (Tehran: Chap-e Sevom, 1362 [1983/84]), pp. 50-55.
6. See "List of Names and Particulars of 10,930 Victims of the Khomeini Regime's Executions," compiled and published by the people's Mujahidin Organization of Iran (Washington), 1984. The government figures, of course, are much lower.
7. Most of the Tudeh leadership was arrested.

8. Eric Rouleau reflects this thinking in his " Khomeini's Iran," *Foreign Affairs*, vol. 59, no. 1 (Fall 1980).

9. For an analysis of the factional picture, see Richard W. Cottam, "Khomeini, the Future and US Options," Policy Paper 38, December 1987, The Stanley Foundation (Muscatine, Iowa).

10. Khomeini raised his voice in favor of free debate among those who support the Islamic state. He did so in response to an appeal by Hujjat al-Islam Muhammad Ali Ansari, who wanted to know which of the ideological orientations in Iran was most harmonious with the *sharia*. Khomeini refused to give a judgment and instead called for free debate. Foreign Broadcast Information Service, *Daily Reports—NES* (FBIS-NES), (Washington, DC), November 7, 1988, p. 55-56.

11. Mehdi Hashemi, who was executed in 1987, headed the Liberation Movement's Bureau of the Revolutionary Guard and, as his trial indicated, acted very much on his own. FBIS-NES, August 18, 1987, p. S-6.

12. Dilip Hiro has a useful summary account of elections in the Islamic Republic. See Hiro, *Iran Under the Ayatollahs*, p. 260.

13. FBIS-South Asia (SAS), October 29, 1985, pp. I 6-7.

14. For the sharpest of these see FBIS-NES, January 7, 1988, pp. 49-50.

15. For an especially interesting picture of the election see "New Elections in Iran Bring in Fewer Ulama in the Majlis," an interview with Kalim Siddiqui, *Crescent International* (Willowdale, Ontario, Canada), June 16-30, 1988.

16. FBIS-NES, June 7, 1988, p. 57.

17. FBIS-NES, September 13, 1988, pp. 55-56.

18. A most revealing speech by Tariq Aziz concerning Iran's military position is reprinted in Tariq Ismael, *Iraq and Iran: Roots of the Conflict* (Syracuse, NY: Syracuse University Press, 1983), pp. 89-100.

19. The opposition in the Kurdish area is the most serious and has taken the form of insurrection led by Abdul Rahman Qassemlu.

20. For development of this point see Cottam, *Iran and the United States*, chapter 5.

21. See for example the statement of the Sunni-dominated Islamic Conference Organization in November 1987. FBIS-NES, November 10, 1987, p. 58-59.

22. This view is commonly expressed by Iranian professors, but the evidence is largely negative, i.e., a lack of any spontaneous demonstrations in Iran's elite universities, the locus of much anti-government activity in the royal dictatorship period.

23. See a bemused editorial page comment in the *New York Times* following the editor's conversations with Iranian exiles. "Iranian Paranoia," *New York Times*, March 8, 1980.

24. See Abol Hasan Bani-Sadr, *Khianat dar Amid* (Betrayal of Hope) (Paris: 1984). He summarizes groups opposing oppression, pp. 50-145.

25. For a further discussion of this see Cottam, " Khomeini, the Future and US Options," p. 9.

26. Evidence of the public dismay can be seen even in the "phone-in" programs on Tehran Radio. See for example FBIS-NES, March 29, 1988, p. 60.

27. Hashemi-Rafsanjani's statement to this effect is particularly interesting. FBIS-NES, July 18, 1988, p. 51.

28. This theme was increasingly emphasized in the months following the cease-fire. See for example the Friday prayer statement of Hashemi-Rafsanjani. FBIS-NES, November 7, 1988, pp. 60-64.

29. See remarks from the March 1988 Islamic Conference Organization meeting in _Al-Dustur_ (Amman). FBIS-NES, March 29, 1988, pp. 4-5.

30. The one real success for the Iranians is to be found in Lebanon. There Sunni and Druze leaders have joined with Shi'i leaders to support the Iranian regime. For examples of all-Muslim cooperation and their pro-Iranian positions, see FBIS-NES, September 23, 1988, p. 27; FBIS-NES, October 14, 1988, pp. 37-38; and FBIS-NES, November 3, 1988, pp. 36-37.

31. Again, the most articulate advocate of this position is Hashemi-Rafsanjani. FBIS-NES, October 19, 1988, p. 56.

32. _Kayhan_, September 22, 1988. FBIS-NES, October 6, 1988, p. 53.

33. Khomeini's lengthy instructions must have pleased both ideological orientations. FBIS-NES, October 4, 1988, p. 46.

34. The decision seemed almost casual. It was announced in the middle of an interview with Hashemi-Rafsanjani on June 4, 1987. FBIS-NES, June 10, 1987, pp. S 9-10.

The Politics of Land, Law, and Social Justice in Iran

Shaul Bakhash

In October 1986 the Iranian Majlis approved a bill to transfer owner-ship of so-called temporary cultivation agricultural land from the owners to the cultivators actually working the land.[1] Temporary culti-vation was a term assigned to land that had been seized by peasants and by revolutionary organizations in the immediate aftermath of the revolution. The government subsequently issued decrees assigning these lands—totalling between 700,000 and 750,000 hectares—to the cultivators on a temporary basis, pending final settlement of the thou-sands of ownership disputes that had resulted from the seizures.[2] The bill of October 1986 to regularize the status of these lands aroused heated debate in the Majlis. It was approved only by a narrow margin on a contested vote. The Council of Guardians (a body of senior Is-lamic jurists and experts on Islamic law) eventually approved the mea-sure; but the Majlis in the course of its deliberation had to revise sev-eral of the bill's provisions in anticipation of Council objections, on Islamic grounds, to the law.

The debate over the temporary cultivation bill sheds considerable light on the vexed problem of land tenure and land reform in the Is-lamic Republic. The controversy regarding this legislation is used in this chapter to address a number of other issues that engaged the atten-tion of Iran's leaders in the first decade after the 1979 Islamic revolu-tion. Among these were the application of Islamic law to matters of public policy, the means of realizing the goal of social justice, the authority of the Majlis or the Council of Guardians to decide such matters, the role of Ayatollah Ruhollah Khomeini as the legitimator of major policy decisions, and the practicalities of parliamentary politics.

Land Seizures

The problem of temporary cultivation arose from the widespread land seizures that occurred following the revolution.[3] The provisional government and the revolutionary prosecutor in Tehran ordered the expropriation of the property of numerous prominent individuals with links to the previous regime or charged with crimes and other activities considered reprehensible by the revolutionaries. Revolutionary courts in the provinces, often without authorization from Tehran, acted in similar fashion. In some instances landlords sought to take advantage of the general disorder in the country and the weakening of central authority to recover land they had lost under the shah's land reform program. They used this opportunity to register in their own names disputed land and land in the public domain.

Widespread seizures of land were also initiated by the villagers themselves. They were often encouraged or led in these seizures by left-wing political groups, such as the Fada'i-e Khalq, the Kurdish Democratic Party (KDP), and the Turkoman People's Movement. Agencies of the revolutionary government frequently participated in these seizures or confirmed them once they had taken place. This activity was greatly accelerated following the approval of a sweeping land reform law enacted by the Revolutionary Council in April 1980. The law envisaged the break-up of all but the smallest landholdings and their distribution to landless or land-poor peasants. It established a central staff for land transfers and local, seven-man committees to administer distribution. These committees began to take over private land and to transfer it to villagers. Moreover, the law appears to have galvanized both the peasants and the various revolutionary and government organizations to take over land and to assign it to cultivators. In addition to the central staff and the seven-man committees, a large number of organizations were involved in these land transfers. The following, gleaned from remarks during debate in the Majlis by various deputies, is only a partial listing: the Revolutionary Guards, the Crusade for Reconstruction, the Foundation for the Disinherited, the Ministry of Agriculture, provincial governors, provincial *'ulama*, magistrates' courts and revolutionary courts, and political movements such as the KDP and Komaleh in Kurdistan, the Turkoman People's movement in Gorgan, and the Saqqafi Center in Khuzistan.[4]

Thus, in addition to land expropriated under laws approved by the Revolutionary Council, rulings handed down by the Tehran revolutionary court, and estates taken over under the April 1980 land reform law, lands were seized by peasants and revolutionary organizations without sanction from the central government. To deal with the disorder and landlord-peasant disputes resulting from these seizures, the Supreme Judicial Council issued a decree in September 1980 that left cultivation of disputed land in the hands of those who had cultivated the land in the previous year, pending a final settlement. This decree, which led to leasing agreements between cultivators and various revolutionary and government organizations, was renewed on an annual basis in 1981 and 1982. In 1983, in a letter to the chief justice, Ayatollah Khomeini once again gave his personal imprimatur to this practice and ordered that cultivators' leases be renewed on an annual basis until the Majlis passed legislation to determine the final ownership. The lands farmed under these decrees thus came to be known as temporary cultivation land.

The Land Distribution Law

By 1986 the general problem of land tenure and land reform, as well as the problem of temporary cultivation land, weighed heavily on the government. Despite an extensive land-distribution program undertaken under the Pahlavi regime and limited measures enforced by the Khomeini government, land ownership remained skewed. Approximately 33.5 percent of cultivators owned only 2 percent, while 0.6

percent of landowners owned 13.2 percent of the arable land in the country. About 10,000 owners held more than 100 hectares each, while 1.6 million held less than 5 hectares each.[5] Although only a limited amount of land had been distributed under the land reform law of April 1980, the law proved controversial and its implementation extremely disruptive. It was suspended by Khomeini, on the advice of his lieutenants, in November of that year.

A more limited land reform law was approved by the Majlis in January 1983 but was vetoed by the Council of Guardians. No major land reform measure was approved by the legislature after this date. Thus, despite numerous promises to the farmers, by 1986 the government had in fact distributed little land to farmers—far less than had been distributed under the much maligned monarchy—and it was still without a land reform program. Debate over land reform, however, had continued virtually unabated. There was considerable sentiment in favor of land distribution in the cabinet, the Majlis, the revolutionary organizations, and among villagers in the countryside. Opposition came from landowners, the bazaar, and the more conservative senior clerics. Individuals on both sides were persuaded that agriculture would continue to suffer as long as the government's intentions regarding land ownership remained unclear, leaving landowners and cultivators insecure in their tenures.

The land distributed under temporary cultivation decrees represented a particularly pressing problem. Although not extensive, the amount of land comprised around 5 percent of all arable land in the country[6] and a much larger proportion of the arable land still in the hands of the larger landowners. Somewhat more than 120,000 farm families had received land—a measure of the disruption that would result from any effort to return the land to the owners. Between 5,000 and 5,600 owners had been dispossessed; these included a number of individuals owning several thousand hectares of land and larger numbers owning several hundred hectares of land each.[7] In addition to the land taken over under the temporary cultivation decrees, these 5,000-plus landowners continued, collectively, to have direct control over another 114,000 hectares of land.

In some cases, the remaining individual holdings were again considerable. For example in Fars, Gholamreza Hakimi lost 800 hectares to temporary cultivation but held on to another 1,200 hectares, while the Behbahani sisters lost 250 hectares to temporary cultivation and held on to another 1,750 hectares.[8] It appears, however, that there were also numerous landlords with small and middle-sized holdings whose land had been seized. In Fars, for example, "occupied" landholders complained they were unjustly being depicted as "feudalists" and large owners; they claimed that they owned only modest amounts of land.[9] Seventy-eight percent of the landowners were absentee with just under 9 percent living in the areas where their land was located. The rest lived only part of the year in rural areas, were abroad, or were owners whose places of residence were unknown.[10]

The bulk of the land seized—and now being cultivated by peasants under the temporary cultivation decrees—was located in seven provinces, of which Mazandaran (primarily the Gonbad and Gorgan districts), with 130,000 hectares, had the highest percentage of confiscated land, followed by Kurdistan (95,000 hectares) and Khuzistan. The incidence of such land was also high in Fars, East Azarbayjan, and the Hamadan and Zanjan districts.[11] Somewhat more than 44 percent of the land had been seized by the cultivators themselves, and nearly 56 percent had been taken over by revolutionary and government organizations and then transferred to the peasants.[12] A small amount of the total, 6.2 percent (or roughly 43,000 hectares), had remained in the hands of revolutionary organizations, but even this was being cultivated by peasants under various leasing arrangements reached with the authorities.[13]

A bill to deal with these lands was presented to the Majlis as a private members' bill in April 1986 and, after review and revision by the Majlis judicial committee, was reported to the full house in October. After intense debates lasting nearly a week, it was enacted into law on October 30, 1986.[14] In its final form, the law provided that ownership of agricultural land throughout the country, which as of March 20, 1981 was in the hands of non-owner cultivators, would be transferred permanently to the cultivators, provided they were landless or land-poor, lacked an adequate source of income other than agriculture, and were resident in the locality. (In Kurdistan, where the disorders resulting from land seizures continued much longer, the effective cut-off date was exceptionally extended to March 20, 1983). Landowners, whose land had been occupied and who were themselves needy and lacked other sources of income, were allowed to keep up to three times the amount of land that was considered necessary in each locality for the maintenance of a rural family. Cultivators dispossessed to provide for needy landowners were to be given land elsewhere. Dispossessed landowners were to be paid "fair value" for their land after the deduction of legal debts and unpaid *shar'i*, or religious, dues. Cultivators receiving land were to pay for their land in installments and would receive full title after payment of the last installment.

The original draft bill had made a much more limited provision for "needy" landlords; the amount of land to be returned to them was increased at the insistence of deputies favoring landlord interests. The undertaking to provide dispossessed cultivators with land "elsewhere" probably had little practical value, given the paucity of arable land in the country. There is also some question as to whether the undertaking to pay owners "fair value" for land transferred to cultivators provided much reassurance to the landholders, in light of the requirement that legal debts and religious dues owed by the landowners must first be settled. Some deputies held that religious dues were voluntary contributions under Islamic law and could not be forcibly collected. But the rapporteur on the bill, Ismail Shushtari, gave an unusually broad interpretation of shar'i dues. They included not only the traditional *khoms* and *zakat*, he said, but any debt for which there was not a legal document and even "debts" incurred as a result of landlord exploitation of cultivators.[15] This interpretation of "religious dues" did not go unchallenged, but the import of the requirement to pay these dues was nevertheless left vague in the final version of the bill. That the article was retained illustrates both the propensity to attempt to legislate on the basis of Islamic law and the persisting disagreement among the leaders of the Islamic Republic over the correct interpretation of the law.

Nevertheless, the law on these temporary lands was actuated, above all, by practical considerations. Unlike the abortive land reform laws of April 1980 and January 1983, it did not aim at comprehensive land distribution. In fact, the law specifically excluded from any benefits all cultivators working land under legally binding rental, crop-sharing, or other tenancy agreements with landowners. Thus, one of the ironies of the law, as its opponents were quick to point out, was that it rewarded those cultivators who had participated in land seizures but made no provision for those cultivators who had continued to honor their prerevolution leasing agreements with landowners. The law aimed at settling the status of a limited, if still significant, amount of land that had been subjected to unauthorized seizure and whose ultimate disposal had remained undetermined. The land in question had been under temporary cultivation for six years. Cultivators, however, still lacked security of tenure, and the owners had kept pressing to get their land back.

In rulings issued in 1982 and 1983, provincial courts had often decided these land disputes in favor of the deed holders. To prevent the ejection of the cultivators or "occupiers," the Supreme Judicial Council had ordered the courts to stop ruling on these cases pending a comprehensive settlement. The uncertainty over ownership meant that neither the owners nor the cultivators were inclined to invest in the land. This situation was especially serious in such areas as Gonbad, where large-scale cotton cultivation was practiced and where maintenance of wells and canals required collective efforts by local landowners or cultivators. Minister of Agriculture Abbas Ali Zali reported in October 1986 that the majority of wells in the Gonbad region were either neglected or ruined and that water canals were in disrepair. Although cotton production had recovered somewhat from the steep decline suffered in the immediate aftermath of the revolution, in 1986 it still stood at an average of 2.8 tons per hectare as against an average of 3.5 tons per hectare achieved before the revolution. In Gorgan, Mazandaran, Khuzistan, and Kurdistan, the minister said that necessary work on dikes, flood control, and water-collection facilities was not being undertaken.[16]

The chairman of the judicial committee, Shushtari, when reporting the bill to the floor of the Majlis, and Zali, when defending it, argued primarily from practicality. Although the bill itself required landlords (or cultivators) to prove their legal title to the land in instances where ownership was in dispute, Shushtari did not in principle question the landlords' legal right to the land. He focused, rather, on the impracticality of attempting to eject 120,000 farming families from land they had been cultivating for several years. Various speakers repeatedly recalled the unsettled conditions prevailing in the aftermath of the revolution to make the point that the land seizures had resulted from general revolutionary turmoil rather than deliberate intention by peasants or revolutionary organizations to engage in "illegal" seizures. The question of intention, as we shall see, was significant because it touched on matters of Islamic law. In emphasizing the postrevolution turmoil in which the land seizures had taken place, however, deputies were also arguing that the temporary cultivation bill was intended to resolve a dilemma deriving from conditions that were outside the government's control. The principle of *zarurat*, or "overriding necessity," under which the bill was introduced, and the compensation provisions of the bill were a further acknowledgment that the government would often be dispossessing those who had legal title to the land, but that it was doing so because the alternative was even less satisfactory.

The practical intentions of the majority of the legislators are also evident from proposals from the floor of the Majlis that in the course of the debate were rejected or incorporated into the bill. The Majlis, for example, took cognizance of the fact that many cultivators (in Gonbad, for instance) were recent migrants, that some landowners who would be allowed to keep land would continue to cultivate through tenants, that many farm families earned part of their income working in nearby towns and cities, and that there was considerable movement of labor between village and town. The Majlis thus rejected attempts to restrict recipients of land to long-term residents in each district, to impose other, narrowly defined residential requirements on recipients, to demand that they cultivate the land they received themselves, and to prevent recipients from subsequently selling their land. The majority of deputies repeatedly opted for flexibility and for accommodation to the varied work and the residential and migratory patterns that characterized Iran's agricultural areas.

Land Reform

Nevertheless, the bill raised larger issues. The Majlis deputies debated with a sense that they were standing at a historic crossroads where fundamental questions of Islamic law, social justice, and property rights were engaged. "If we approve something in violation of Islamic law," Muhammad Baqer Akhundi, one of the deputies, said, "it is as if each day we commit a million sins."[17] Both supporters and opponents saw the proposed law as a precedent-setting measure. If for one group of deputies the passage of the bill would signify the Islamic Republic's commitment to the cause of the disinherited, to another group the measure had a more sinister implication: "The only purpose of this bill," said Seyyed Ahmad Kashani, "is to undermine [the principle of] ownership in our society."[18]

Both sides drew on Islamic law and on Khomeini's interpretations of Islamic law to buttress their arguments. The opponents of the bill argued on the basis of property rights, the illegal nature of the land seizures, and the lack, as they saw it, of any urgency for drastic action.

The advocates of the bill sought to develop an argument in its favor based on the founding principles of the Islamic Republic, a doctrine of fairness, and civil order. They used the debate for an all-out attack on the landowning classes. In this they employed a rhetoric, widespread since the revolution, that contrasts the supposed moral corruption and exploitative nature of the rich with the nobility and goodness of the poor, the negative qualities of urban life (associated with the rich) with the simplicity of rural life (associated with the poor). They depicted the landowners as exploiters of the peasantry and plunderers of the country, loyalists of the old regime and partners in its corruption, and as men lacking devotion to the revolution or to agriculture. Thus, Deputy Hoseyn Harati described the majority of the landowners as "khans and feudalists [who] quit this country at the very dawn of the revolution and departed in fear, due to the crimes they had committed." The peasants live and toil on the land, he said, while the landlords "live in the cities, in villas and apartments, drive luxury, latest-model cars and benefit from the fruit of the labor of the unfortunate farmer and villager."[19]

In the same vein, Ali Movahedi-Savuji attributed the flight of the landowners from the rural areas to their "moral corruption or the oppression they had practiced in the region." They had not been forcibly expelled from their lands, he asserted, "they themselves were afraid to return."[20] According to another deputy, the dispossessed landlords were not legitimate owners at all. They were all "khans" and "little Shahs."[21] Other deputies argued that the property takeovers were justified because the landowners had acquired their holdings through questionable means. For example, Sadeq Khalkhali asserted that most of the owners in Gonbad had secured their land as a result of huge bank loans and other favors extended by the old regime. According to Minister of Agriculture Zali, the same held true for lands acquired before the revolution in Khuzistan and Kurdistan. Qanbar Kabiri argued that no one could have amassed several thousand hectares of land without exploiting farmers and the deprived classes; in other words, excessive wealth was itself an indication of wrongful acquisition. According to Deputy Harati, the government had a right to take the land in compensation for the monies, to which the state no longer had access, that the departed landowners had looted from the country before the revolution.[22]

The assumption that the landlords had exploited the peasants in the past and would do so in the future was implicit in the remarks of many supporters of the bill. Several predicted disorder in the countryside if the landlords were allowed to return. "The return of these khans to the villages will give birth to corruption, will create conflict, will generate problems for the Islamic Republic," said Mohsen Rahami.[23] "Do you want to bring them back . . . to [again] make the khans and feudalists the overlords?" asked Harati.[24]

Besides, according to these deputies, the peasants had readily sacrificed their lives, the lives of their sons, and their meager property to Islam and the revolution; the landlords had made no sacrifices for the revolutionary cause. In this sense, the peasants were seen as the deserving classes, the true devotees of Islam and the revolution. The peasants had borne the burden of fighting the war with Iraq, and year after year brought in their harvests to support the war effort. "For seven years," said Harati, "the cultivator, with his work-hardened hands, has toiled and shed sweat and suffered deprivation," while the landlords had done nothing.[25] "How many of the children of these landowners, for whom the gentlemen beat their breasts and on whom they expend so much energy, are at the front? How many have themselves gone?" asked Fazel Harandi.[26] Shushtari echoed him: "What have the landlords done about the revolution, about the war?"[27]

Another supporter of the bill, Ibrahim Islami, also drew a sharp contrast between peasant and landlord attitudes toward the revolution and made a plea for an Islam devoted to the cause of the poor: "Today, the defenders of the revolution are the cultivators. The defenders of Islam are the cultivators; and the khans . . . strike blows [against the revolution] by whatever means they can. We must not speak of Islam in a manner as if it came to defend the interests of the powerful."[28] In addition, many deputies saw land distribution as a means of preempting the appeal of the radical left, especially among the younger generation. Sadeq Khalkhali, a supporter of the bill, thus argued that failure to approve the measure would only give ammunition to the enemies of the revolution who were misleading the young by posing as the champions of the deprived classes.[29]

Repeatedly, however, the advocates of land distribution reverted to a concept of fairness that was often explicitly articulated and always implicit in their remarks. It was the *duty* of the Islamic government to take land from the "bullies" or the rich, Kabiri argued, and give it to the "true owners of the land" or the disinherited.[30] For Movahedi-Savuji, the bill was justified on the basis of need. Without the land, the peasants would have no income and for them securing ownership was "a matter of life and death."[31] Shushtari also appealed to a simple criterion of justice. It was not just, he said, for 5,000 landlords to own an average of 160 hectares each and 120,000 cultivators to own no land. Using a rough rule of thumb based on the total amount of land still in the hands of these landlords and the amount that would be transferred to peasant families under the proposed law, he calculated that the landowners would still end up with an average of 20 hectares each while the peasants would end up with an average of no more than 7 hectares each; this, he implied, was more than fair to the landlords.[32] Several speakers ridiculed the idea of taking land away from poor

peasants in order to return it to wealthy landowners. "Protection of
the deprived and the unfortunate was one of the basic demands of this
revolution," said Gholam Reza Haydari, "and the exalted leader has
again and again emphasized this point."[33]

Unable to defeat the bill, deputies opposed to the measure sought
to save as much land as possible for the landowners. They clearly
sensed, however, that the principle of land distribution and the populist rhetoric against the wealthy and for the "disinherited" employed
by the bill's supporters exercised a powerful appeal among important
constituencies. "Now that this discussion is under way in the Majlis,"
said Shushtari, "all the cultivators . . . are on the alert to see what their
representatives are going to do. The same is true for the martyr-
nurturing nation."[34] The opponents of the bill thus carefully avoided
identification with the landowning classes and sought to guard against
the charge that they were siding with the landholders against the landless peasants. "The nation, [and] the world should know," said Abu
Taleb Mahmudi-Golpaygani, "we are defending *legitimate* ownership.
Non-legitimate ownership, and the property of the Shah, the executed
and the fugitives—may God curse them—this must be returned to its
rightful owners."[35] "There is not a single honorable member of the
Majlis who sides with the khan," added Muhammad Ali Movahedi-
Kermani.[36]

The opponents of the bill challenged the depiction of those whose
lands had been seized as feudal khans. They asserted that many of the
landowners were themselves small holders dependent for their liveli-
hoods on their holdings. They depicted the cultivators not as exploited
peasants with legitimate grievances that must be satisfied but as avari-
cious usurpers who deserved to be expelled from land they had illegally seized. They warned that passage of the bill would undermine
business confidence and the propensity to invest and would lead to
a flight of capital. "I state clearly," said Mahmudi-Golpaygani, "that
our economy is being crippled. Economic insecurity is visiting frightening problems on this country. They [businessmen, investors] are taking away the gold. They are taking away the wealth. They say it is
impossible to do business in this country."[37] Again and again the opponents of the bill reverted to the rights of property under Islamic law.

The landowners whom the law proposed to dispossess, they asserted, had for the most part acquired their property through inheritance, investment, or revival of waste land—that is, in a manner that establishes legitimate ownership under Islamic law; and Islamic law did not permit tampering with legitimate property. If the land under dispute had been illegally acquired, they said, then this must be established before a court of law and on a case by case basis. Legitimate ownership could not be nullified by an all-encompassing statute. The debate on the temporary cultivation bill, like the discussion of other measures touching on private property that had come up before the Majlis, thus became a debate on matters of Islamic jurisprudence. In this instance the debate also centered on the applicability of the doctrine of zarurat to the land question.

Implications of Islamic Jurisprudence

The doctrine of zarurat has a long history in Islamic jurisprudence. The doctrine holds that the primary rulings of Islam may be temporarily waived in emergencies or conditions of overriding necessity. Traditionally, the concept of zarurat has been applied primarily to personal cases, to exigencies affecting the individual believer. For example, the prohibition against the consumption of pork might be waived for a Muslim facing starvation. As developed and articulated by Khomeini and others since the Iranian Revolution, the doctrine of overriding necessity has been applied to broad societal issues and broad questions of social justice. It has been argued, for instance, that the doctrine of overriding necessity may be invoked to waive the primary rulings of Islam if the very existence of the state is threatened or, in Khomeini's words, in instances where inaction would lead to "wickedness and corruption."[38]

The doctrine was initially invoked as a means out of the impasse reached between the Majlis and the Council of Guardians on a number of social welfare and economic measures (such as nationalization of foreign trade, land distribution, and confiscation of the property of emigrés) approved by the Majlis but vetoed by the Council of

Guardians as violating Islamic principles. In October 1981 Khomeini
suggested that the Majlis could approve measures it considered essential for the life of the community but which seemed in conflict with
Islamic principles on the basis of overriding necessity. It turned out,
however, that the Majlis and the Council of Guardians could not agree
on the conditions that justified recourse to the principle of zarurat.

In January 1983 Khomeini ruled that the Majlis could make a convincing case for invoking the doctrine of overriding necessity by ap-
proving measures deemed to be in conflict with Islamic law by a two-
thirds majority.[39] The so-called two-thirds principle was subsequently
used sparingly, but not always successfully, to anticipate or override
the Council of Guardians' objections to items of legislation. Because
the Council of Guardians had in the past almost invariably vetoed
laws that tampered with what it considered legitimately acquired private property, the Majlis was aware that overriding necessity would
have to be invoked if the temporary cultivation bill was to have any
chance of passing muster with the Council. The temporary cultivation
bill was therefore presented under the rubric of overriding necessity.

Proponents argued that the legislation was essential to preserve the
very order of the Islamic Republic and the fundamental principles of
social justice on which the whole edifice stood. The farmers, said Fazel
Harandi, a supporter of the bill, had long been promised a satisfactory
resolution to the land question. If they were disappointed once again,
he suggested, disorder might result. The villagers might grow indiffer-
ent and lose faith in the system. Because the farmers and their sons
manned the fronts in the war with Iraq, their indifference could lead
to military disaster. Failure to give tenant cultivators the land, said
Harati, would leave 120,000 farmers and their families, 900,000 people altogether by his calculation, without a source of income. They
would all migrate to the cities. "To make 120,000 persons jobless,"
said Kabiri, "will create unemployment and undermine the system."[40]
The return of the landowners to their lands after an absence of several
years, according to others, would play havoc with agriculture and create precisely the disorder that Khomeini had warned against.

Deputies arguing in support of the temporary cultivation bill tended
to conflate the doctrine of overriding necessity with the claim regard-

ing the allegedly illicit manner in which landlords had acquired land. The two arguments, however, derived from very different premises. As many deputies pointed out, the invocation of the doctrine of overriding necessity assumed *legitimate* ownership, thus requiring a temporary suspension of principles of Islamic law. Overriding necessity need not be invoked at all, they noted, if the owners had come by their property illegitimately.

The arguments of the proponents of the bill also suggest a broad interpretation of the doctrine of overriding necessity, variously invoked here in the name of social order, economic well-being, the promise of the revolution, the cultivators' faith in Islam and the simple need to resolve a difficulty resulting from revolutionary events.[41] It is also an interpretation that shades into concepts of the "social good," social justice, and fairness touched on earlier.

The opponents of the bill leaned toward a narrow interpretation of zarurat. They drew on Islamic jurisprudence to argue that overriding necessity could not be invoked when Islamic principles had been violated to bring about the very exigency that required resolution or when the beneficiaries deliberately created a situation of crisis and acted from reprehensible motives. The peasants who had seized land, said Fahim Kermani, "threw themselves on the property of the people with full envy, greed and appetite." They were "rebels and wrongdoers, and therefore zarurat does not apply to them." They had committed acts that were "contrary to the *shari'a* and impermissible . . . and no one, let alone an Islamic jurist or student [of the law] will say, 'this property is illegitimate; come and take it'."[42] It was to refute the allegation that the peasants acted out of greed and in full awareness that they were engaging in wrongful acts that supporters of the bill stressed the disturbed conditions prevailing in the aftermath of the revolution. Similarly they emphasized the encouragement, by word and example, that government organizations had given the cultivators to occupy the land and cultivate it.

Both the narrow and the broad interpreters of the doctrine of overriding necessity sought support for their views in rulings and statements by Khomeini. But Khomeini, it turned out, had spoken in favor both of social justice and of a strict interpretation of Islamic law. He had denigrated the large landowners as exploiters of the peasantry and also warned against unlawful attacks on private property, had approved the 1980 land reform law and then suspended it, had sided at times with the Council of Guardians and the narrow interpreters and at other times with the Majlis and the broad interpreters on matters of property and Islamic law. He had endorsed the use of the principle of overriding necessity in the broader interests of the community, but he did not consistently support the implications of such a position. Khomeini's rulings and views, in other words, although considered authoritative, lent themselves to varying interpretations.

The invocation of the principle of zarurat confronted powerful Majlis Speaker Ali Akbar Hashemi-Rafsanjani, a supporter of the bill, with a dilemma. Hashemi-Rafsanjani was aware that only under the rubric of overriding necessity was there a chance that the Council of Guardians would not block the temporary cultivation measure. He was not certain, however, that he could muster a two-thirds majority for the bill, and he engaged in a considerable amount of parliamentary maneuvering to avoid a two-thirds vote or to blur its import. Thus the controversy that characterized the debate spilled over into the voting on the bill. Hashemi-Rafsanjani initially took the position that a two-thirds vote was not necessary on the first reading (when the deputies voted on the broad generalities of the bill), but only on those clauses where some principle of Islamic law was involved and in danger of being violated.

When deputies opposed to the bill forced an initial vote on the two-thirds issue, the speaker took a voice vote only and, over the protests of many deputies, asserted that two-thirds had voted in favor. During the debate, he repeatedly skirmished with opponents of the bill who charged he was trying to silence them. He also took the position that if the Majlis approved the bill as a matter of overriding exigency by a two-thirds vote, then the Council of Guardians would be bound by the decision and could not refer the bill back to the legislature. In fact, this was by no means a settled issue between the legislature and the Council. There had been occasions in the past when bills approved by a two-thirds vote in the Majlis were rejected by the Council of Guardians or returned to the deputies for revision.

On the final vote, Hashemi-Rafsanjani refused the demand of some deputies for a secret (written) ballot and asked deputies to indicate, by rising, their approval (or disapproval) of the bill. There were 190 members present. Two officers of the Majlis counted the yes votes (the no vote was never recorded); one of the officers reported 142 in favor and the other reported 130 in favor. Although the discrepancy between the two counts was considerable, Hashemi-Rafsanjani refused shouted demands for a recount. By his calculation, 125 votes constituted a two-thirds majority. In a tumultuous ending to the session with opponents of the bill calling for a recount and supporters claiming victory, Hashemi-Rafsanjani declared the temporary cultivation law approved.[43]

Conclusion

Several conclusions can be drawn from the debate over the temporary cultivation bill and its eventual outcome. Since the revolution, a populist rhetoric regarding social justice and a more egalitarian distribution of wealth has gained sufficient popularity and acceptance that no deputy wished to be identified as a defender of the rich or the propertied interests. The deputies opposed to the bill were sensitive to the media focus on the debate. In the closing moments of the debate, they proved reluctant to stand up and be counted as opponents of the bill. Their demand for a secret ballot derived from a desire for anonymity and from an expectation that a larger number would vote against the bill if they did not have to do so publicly.[44]

At the same time, sentiment in favor of property—whether out of concern for property owners or out of concern for the specifics of Islamic law as understood by opponents of the measure—remained considerable in the Second Majlis and could not be entirely overlooked. Opponents of land distribution were unable to muster enough votes to defeat the bill, but they did manage to increase the amount of land that would be left in the possession of "needy" landowners and to secure other modifications of the bill. Moreover, Hashemi-Rafsanjani had to rush through the "two-thirds" votes because he was not confident that he could muster the necessary majorities for the controversial bill. The approval of the bill on a three-year "trial" basis remained a transparent device to win grudging Council of Guardian acquiescence in the permanent transfer of legitimately acquired property.

The debate over the temporary cultivation bill emphasizes once again the centrality of the concept of property rights in all discussions of social justice in the Islamic Republic. Repeatedly, it is issues touching on property and the state's power to tamper with private property that have aroused the strongest sentiments among the religious leaders. The controversy also reflects the inability of Iran's religious and secular leaders to agree on interpretations of Islamic law that can simultaneously satisfy the concern for social justice and the concern for property rights as articulated by different factions and individuals within the leadership. Khomeini often used strong language against the propertied classes and in favor of the disinherited and at times claimed almost unlimited powers that allow the Islamic state to intervene in the private sector in the wider interests of the community. But his own wavering on this issue reflected wider divisions among influential constituencies in the country, its leaders, and the senior clerical community.

Nor has the attempt to bridge these differences through consultative mechanisms always succeeded. In February 1988, Khomeini named a 13-member "council for determining the interests of the Islamic order," composed of the six jurists of the Council of Guardians, six members from the government and the Majlis, and his personal representative, to resolve differences among the Council, the government, and the Majlis over major items of legislation. The fact that this council has proceeded cautiously is one more indication that divisions within the leadership on issues touching on property and social justice remain deep and that for many senior clerics the attempt to base a policy of distributive justice on the broad principles of Islamic jurisprudence remains problematical.

It is also clear that a new vocabulary and new interpretations of Islamic traditions touching on matters of social justice are, however, becoming part of current political discourse. Since the revolution, Iran's clerics have most often depicted themselves as champions of the disinherited classes, have not willingly identified with men of property, and have chosen to forget periods in recent history when they took a different stand. During the debate on the temporary cultivation bill, however, Mahmudi-Golpaygani recalled that in the 1960s the 'ulama, almost to a man, opposed the shah's land reform program. "At the time of the land reform of the Shah," he said, ". . . all the ulama, the hojjat al-Islams, the high ayatollahs, the lower-level propagators of the holy law, all [preached] from the pulpits, wrote, and said that [land distribution] is forbidden, is equivalent to struggle against the Imam of the Age."[45] Such a vocabulary continues to be employed, albeit with greater circumspection, in the Islamic Republic; but it competes, as we have seen, with a vocabulary and an interpretation of Islamic law that is sharply different in its assumptions and its implications.

NOTES

1. A primary source for this article is the official record of Majlis debates. These are found in *Ruznameh-ye Rasmi-ye Jomhuri-ye Islami-ye Iran: Mashruh-e Mozakerat-e Majles-e Showra-ye Islami* (Official Gazette of the Islamic Republic of Iran: Proceedings of the Islamic Consultative Assembly), hereafter cited as *Proceedings*, published in Tehran by the Ministry of Justice. At times the nearest equivalent Christian year is used for the Iranian year. Thus the Iranian year 1360 appears in the text as 1981 rather than as 1981-82.

2. The total amount of land involved was variously cited by officials and Majlis deputies as 700,000, 720,000, and 750,000 hectares. A hectare is equivalent to 2.5 acres. See *Proceedings*, 29 Mehr 1365 (October 21, 1986), statements by Ismail Shustari, p. 24; *ibid.*, 1 Aban 1365 (October 23, 1986), statements by Muhammad Ali Movahedi-Savuji and Shustari, pp. 23, 27; *ibid.*, 6 Aban 1365 (October 28, 1986), statements by Qanbar Kabiri, p. 21.

3. For background on the land issue and land reform legislation in the Islamic Republic, see Ahmad Ashraf, "Dehqanan, Zamin va Enqelab" (Peasants, Land, and Revolution) in Ashraf (ed.), *Masa'el-e Arzi va Dehqani* (Problems of Land and Peasants) (Tehran: Agah Publications, 1361 [1982]), pp. 50-74; Shaul Bakhash, *Reign of the Ayatollahs: Iran and the Islamic Revolution* (New York: Basic Books, 1984), pp. 195-216; Asghar Schirazi, *The Prob-*

46 *Iran's Revolution*

lem of the Land Reform in the Islamic Republic of Iran: Complications and Consequences of an Islamic Reform Policy (Berlin: Free University of Berlin, 1987).

4. *Proceedings*, 6 Aban 1365 (October 28, 1986), Abol Fazl Musavi-Tabrizi, p. 21; Nabizadeh, p. 23.

5. *Ibid.*, 29 Mehr 1365 (October 21, 1986), Kabiri, p. 31; Schirazi, *Problem of Land Reform*, p. 8.

6. Based on a calculation of 14.9 million hectares of total arable agricultural land in the country. See Schirazi, *Problem of Land Reform*, p. 8.

7. For number of owners see *Proceedings*, 1 Aban 1365 (October 23, 1986), Shushtari, p. 27. Among the individual holdings cited in the parliamentary debates are the following: Fars Province—Delavari, 4,000 hectares; Jalilvand, 4,500 hectares; Mrs. Anbar Behbahani, 3,000 hectares; Muhammad Bayat, 7,000 hectares; Gonbad Province—Qaderi, 2,700 hectares; Ja'farbay, 2,700 hectares; and Komak Shaykhi, 1,800 hectares. *Proceedings*, 1 Aban 1365 (October 23, 1986), Movahedi-Savuji, p. 23.

8. *Ibid.*, Movahedi-Savuji, p. 23.

9. *Ibid.*, 29 Mehr 1365 (October 21, 1986), Seyyed Ahmad Kashani, p. 27.

10. *Ibid.*, 1 Aban 1365 (October 23, 1986), Shushtari, p. 28.

11. *Ibid.*, 29 Mehr 1365 (October 21, 1986), Abbas Ali Zali, p. 26 and 1 Aban 1365 (October 23, 1986), Zali, p. 25; 29 Mehr 1365 (October 21, 1986), Hoseyn Harati, p. 26; 1 Aban 1365 (October 23, 1986), Kabiri, p. 28.

12. *Ibid.*, 6 Aban 1365 (October 28, 1986), Kabiri, p. 21; Nabizadeh, p. 22.

13. *Ibid.*, 7 Aban 1365 (October 29, 1986), p. 29.

14. For the full text of the law, see *Proceedings*, 8 Aban 1365 (October 30, 1986), pp. 30-31.

15. *Ibid.*, 7 Aban 1365 (October 29, 1986), Akrami and Shushtari, p. 27.

16. *Ibid.*, 1 Aban 1365 (October 23, 1986), Zali, pp. 25-26.

17. *Ibid.*, 29 Mehr 1365 (October 21, 1986), Muhammad Baqer Akhundi, p. 25.

18. *Ibid.*, 29 Mehr 1365 (October 21, 1986), Kashani, p. 27.

19. *Ibid.*, 29 Mehr 1365 (October 21, 1986), Harati, pp. 26-27.

20. *Ibid.*, 1 Aban 1365 (October 23, 1986), Movahedi-Savuji, p. 23.

21. *Ibid.*, 7 Aban 1365 (October 29, 1986), Ibrahim Islami on "little Shahs," p. 34.

22. *Ibid.*, 29 Mehr 1365 (October 21, 1986), Sadeq Khalkhali, p. 28; Zali, p. 26; Kabiri, p. 30; Harati, p. 26.

23. *Ibid.*, 7 Aban 1365 (October 29, 1986), Mohsen Rahami, p. 33.

24. *Ibid.*, 29 Mehr 1365 (October 21, 1986), Harati, p. 26.

25. *Ibid.*, 29 Mehr 1365 (October 21, 1986), Harati, p. 26.

26. *Ibid.*, 1 Aban 1365 (October 23, 1986), Fazel Harandi, p. 25.

27. *Ibid.*, Shushtari, p. 23.

28. *Ibid.*, 7 Aban 1365 (October 29, 1986), Ibrahim Islami, p. 35.

29. *Ibid.*, 29 Mehr 1365 (October 21, 1986), Khalkhali, p. 29.

30. *Ibid.*, 29 Mehr 1365 (October 21, 1986), Kabiri, p. 30.

31. *Ibid.*, 1 Aban 1365 (October 23, 1986), Movahedi-Savuji, p. 22.

32. *Ibid.*, 1 Aban 1365 (October 23, 1986), Shushtari, p. 28.

33. *Ibid.*, 7 Aban 1365 (October 29, 1986), Gholam Reza Haydari, p. 28.

34. *Ibid.*, 1 Aban 1365 (October 23, 1986), Shushtari, p. 28.

35. *Ibid.*, 7 Aban 1365 (October 29, 1986), Mahmudi-Golpaygani, p. 31 (emphasis added).

36. *Ibid.*, 8 Aban 1365 (October 30, 1986), Movahedi-Kermani, p. 21.

37. *Ibid.*, 29 Mehr 1365 (October 21, 1986), Mahmudi-Golpaygani, p. 30.

38. See letter to Ali Akbar Hashemi-Rafsanjani, *Kayhan*, 20 Mehr 1360 (October 12, 1981).

39. On the issue of zarurat, see Bakhash, *Reign of the Ayatollahs*, pp. 206-216; and Schirazi, *Problem of Land Reform*, pp. 16-23, 28-33.

40. *Proceedings*, 1 Aban 1365 (October 23, 1986), Harandi, pp. 24-25; 29 Mehr 1365 (October 21, 1986), Harati, p. 26; 1 Aban 1365 (October 23, 1986), Kabiri, p. 28.

41. The possibility that this potentially open-ended concept of overriding necessity could be translated into a justification for almost untrammeled state power is evident from the ruling that Ayatollah Khomeini issued in January 1988. Addressing himself to the differences that had emerged between the Council of Guardians and the government and Majlis over legislation on economic and social justice issues, Khomeini articulated a broad and even unlimited definition of the powers of an Islamic state. He said that such a state derives its powers from "the absolute powers entrusted to the Prophet," and exercises power by divine sanction. In the interests of the community, an Islamic government can, he continued, "unilaterally revoke any agreement with people . . . prevent any matter, whether religious or secular, if it is against the interests of Islam." He added that in the wider interests of the community an Islamic government can even suspend the exercise of the five pillars of the faith, including fasting, prayer, and the pilgrimage to Mecca, whose performance is required of every Muslim. (*Kayhan*, January 7, 1988. Also, see the citation in Bakhash, "Islam and Power Politics," *New York Review of Books*, July 21, 1988, p. 32). Khomeini, however, later retreated somewhat from this extreme formulation.

42. *Proceedings*, 1 Aban 1365 (October 23, 1986), Fahim Kermani, p. 24; see also, *ibid.*, Mojtaba Mir-Ja'fari, p. 22; 6 Aban 1365 (October 28, 1986), Musavi-Tabrizi, p. 21.

43. For an account of the final vote, see *Proceedings*, 8 Aban 1365 (October 28, 1986), pp. 29-31.

44. This is also implicit in Hashemi-Rafsanjani's demand that even on a written ballot, he would require the deputies to put down their names. *Proceedings*, 8 Aban 1365 (October 28, 1986), p. 31.

45. *Proceedings*, 29 Mehr 1365 (October 21, 1986), Mahmud Golpaygani, p. 29. This is probably the first time that the almost universal opposition of the clerics to the land reform program carried out by the previous regime has been stated so explicitly and in a public forum.

Iran's Foreign Policy

CONTENDING ORIENTATIONS

R. K. Ramazani

> Weight not the seat of power with your grandeur
> Unless by deeds you've made the seat secure.
> —Hafiz, 14th century Persian poet
> (author's free adaptation)

An entire decade of cold war and nearly a year of sporadic armed skirmishes between Tehran and Washington have not led to a better US understanding of revolutionary Iran's foreign policy. Academic discussion has helped, but not enough. Two dominant analytical tendencies have impeded a fuller comprehension. One views Iran's foreign policy as though it were a mirror image of its "domestic politics." The other sees Iran's foreign policy mainly in terms of geopolitics. An examination of Iran's words and deeds and its theories and practices makes clear that Tehran's foreign policy has been shaped largely by an acute interplay between its domestic situation, not merely factional politics, and its external environment, not merely superpower behavior.

By taking such a look, this article attempts to enhance the understanding of Iran's foreign policy by identifying, in broad strokes, its main orientations. In doing so, it also endeavors to shed fresh light on some older interpretations about such momentous decisions as to why Iran took US hostages and then took the initiative to free them, or why it continued the war with Iraq when it could have ended it, and then did end it. Finally, this essay will broach the central implications of all this for Iran and the United States.

Twin Revolution

The eruption of the Iranian Revolution in 1978 reflected as much a nationwide opposition to the shah's foreign policy as to his domestic policy. The opposition's attack on his foreign policy centered on his de facto alliance with the United States, and hence the revolutionary epithet, "the American King." Whether the "roots" of the revolution are traceable back to 1953, when the government of Muhammad Mossadegh was destroyed, or to 1963, when the opposition to the shah's regime led by Ayatollah Ruhollah Khomeini was suppressed, or to the society, culture, and politics of an Iran of earlier times, the immediate causes of the revolution lay in the unprecedented ferment of the 1972-77 period, or in what can be described as the "twin revolution of rising alienation" from the shah's regime and from the United States.[1]

Although as early as 1941 when he ascended the throne, the shah had longed to become an "ally" of the United States, and although after the fall of Mossadegh he forged unprecedented economic, political, and military ties with Washington, his de facto alliance with the United States was the byproduct of the 1972-77 era. In 1972, President Richard Nixon promised the shah he could buy any and every category of US conventional military equipment that he wanted. The explosion of oil revenues the following year enabled the shah to buy large quantities of arms; by 1977 he had purchased over $6 billion worth from the United States and had more than $12 billion on order. The shah dreamed of making Iran one of the five conventional military powers of the world, and Washington fueled his ambitions to some extent by anointing his regime the policeman of the Persian Gulf.[2] Many Iranians saw this surrogacy of the shah's regime as a sign of Iran's complete subservience to the United States and its loss of independence. This popular perception developed into a profound source of alienation.[3]

Yet such alienation alone would not have triggered the revolution; there developed an even greater source. The colossal oil-revenue earnings of 1973-74 were accompanied by a spectacular rate of economic growth—43 percent in 1974—an unprecedented budget surplus of $2 billion in the same year, and rising expectations. But almost immediately thereafter the GNP rate fell drastically to 14 percent in 1975, the budget deficit rose dramatically to nearly $6 billion by 1977, and the revolution of rising expectations developed into a revolution of rising alienation. As if the tumultuous social, economic, and psychological dislocations that all this financial boom and bust entailed were not enough, the shah's regime, in 1975, destroyed even the appearance of competitive politics by creating the Rastakhiz Party and demanding allegiance to it. Instead of mobilizing mass support for his regime, this hated party helped provide the mass support base for the disparate sociopolitical forces which finally coalesced in opposition to the shah. Thanks to his modernization efforts of the previous decade, by 1978 half of the Iranian population was urban, and mostly poor. The shah's repressive rule also intensified the underground campaign of assassination against his officials and US military personnel. During this time, while in exile in Najaf, Iraq, Ayatollah Khomeini taught about the anti-Islamic nature of monarchy and the virtues of the rule of the *faqih*.

Nationalist Nonalignment

When Khomeini appointed Mehdi Bazargan as the provisional prime minister on February 5, 1979, the first priority of his government was to terminate the subservient de facto alliance of the shah's regime with the United States and place the relations of the two countries on a plane of "equality." He plotted his foreign policy on the basis of "equilibrium" (*tavazon*), a principle dating back to 1848-1851 when it was first introduced in earnest into Iranian foreign-policy thinking and practice by Mirza Taqi Khan, better known as Amir Kabir, during his short-lived premiership.[4] This principle was the inverse of the European balance-of-power principle. It aimed at maintaining Iran's independence vis-à-vis Britain and Russia—the imperial rivals of greatest concern to Iran at the time—by adopting a policy of "impartiality" (*bitarafi*), or nonalignment. In his book on Amir Kabir, Majlis Speaker Ali Akbar Hashemi-Rafsanjani characterizes him as "the champion of the struggle against colonialism."[5]

Bazargan adopted a nonalignment policy. He believed that Iran's policy toward the Great Powers, to use his words, "should be the same as the policy of (Mossadeq)."[6] Better known as the policy of "negative equilibrium" (*movazeneh-ye manfi*), Mossadegh's nonalignment policy had aimed at maintaining Iran's independence by terminating British domination. Bazargan sought similarly to end America's dominant influence by undoing the shah's de facto alliance with the United States. According to revolutionary Iran's first foreign minister, Karim Sanjabi, Iran's nonalignment policy was based on four pillars: "history, the country's geographic position, the spiritual and humanist ideals of Islam, and the principle of complete reciprocity in relations with other countries."[7]

The reference to Islamic ideals did not mean that either Sanjabi or Bazargan believed, as Khomeini did, that the prime unit of loyalty in the Iranian polity should be Islam. Sanjabi's National Front and Bazargan's Iran Liberation Front were both secular, nationalist, and democratic in nature, drawing their social support largely from the middle classes and the modern-educated intellectuals. For both of them the prime unit of the people's loyalty to polity was considered to be the Iranian nation-state. Bazargan claimed that his movement was a bridge between the secular National Front and the religious movement led by Khomeini. Yet, he knew that he was what could be called an "Iran firster" while Khomeini was an "Islam firster." In Bazargan's own words, "I believe in the service of Iran by means of Islam" while Khomeini "believes in the service of Islam by means of Iran."[8] This profound difference between the two leaders surfaced in a dramatic way at the outbreak of the hostage crisis.

Despite his deep-felt resentment of the Carter administration's continuing support of the shah's regime, Bazargan tried to pursue a nonhostile, nonalignment policy toward the United States. To end the shah's de facto alliance with the United States, on March 12, 1979 Sanjabi withdrew Iran's membership from the Central Treaty Organization (CENTO). More consequentially, on November 3, Foreign

Minister Ibrahim Yazdi canceled the Iranian-US defense agreement of
March 5, 1959. To overturn the shah's de facto alliance more substan-
tively required the overhauling of a complex web of military relationships with the United States built up over the years by the shah. This
overhauling involved such issues as the disposition of the $12 billion
worth of arms on order, the security of some 80 American-built F-14s,
and the disbanding of two secret US listening bases near the Soviet
border.

On the same day that the Bazargan government canceled Iran's defense agreement with the United States, it also abrogated Articles V
and VI of Iran's 1921 treaty with the Soviet Union. After the November 6, 1979 resignation of Bazargan, this cancellation was affirmed
on November 10 by the Revolutionary Council. The Soviet Union
claims that these articles give it the unilateral right to intervene in Iran
militarily whenever it judges that its security is threatened from Iranian territory.[9] These nefarious articles have been repeatedly invoked
by the Soviet Union as a means of pressuring Tehran whenever Moscow believes that Iran is tilting westward. Reza Shah secretly tried to
cancel them in 1935, and his son did the same in 1958-59, but to date
the Soviet Union refuses to do so.

Sanjabi told the Soviet Union in no uncertain terms that Iran had
"bad memories" of its relations with its northern neighbor. He said
that, "our country genuinely wants friendly relations with the USSR,
and it will refuse to be [the base] for attack or propaganda against
it. . . . On the other hand, we will not allow recurrence of disturbing
precedents such as requests for oil concessions, territorial demands or
proclamation of the Kurdish Republic at Mahabad. We will defend
Iran's independence, integrity and unity whatever the cost."[10]

Idealistic Confrontation

The seizure of the US Embassy on November 4, 1979 and the
444-day hostage dispute that followed became the crucible of an idealistic revolutionary foreign policy that set Iran against much of the rest
of the world. Bazargan's nonalignment policy was nationalistic and

accommodational, based on the historic principle of equilibrium. As such, it sought to maintain Iran's independence within the context of the existing international system of nation-states. The new idealistic revolutionary orientation in essence defied that system, its norms of diplomatic behavior, and its international law. It was based on a radical interpretation of Khomeini's transnational ideal of what this author terms an "Islamic world order." The "student-captors" of the US hostages were the original architects of this confrontational foreign policy, an orientation that continues to date within the ruling political elite and certain non-elite factions of Iranian political culture.

The takeover of the US Embassy in part reflected the culmination of the opposition of extremist factions to the moderates at the center. Extremists at opposite poles of the political spectrum attacked Bazargan's policy of nonalignment, accusing him and his foreign ministers of pro-Americanism. It was no coincidence that only three days after the seizure of power by revolutionary forces, the US Embassy was attacked for the first time. The common bond of opposition to the shah that had held the disparate sociopolitical forces together, however, became unglued during the seizure of power from the shah on February 11, 1979. After a couple of days, US Ambassador William Sullivan and some other Americans were freed as a result of intervention by Ibrahim Yazdi and others in Khomeini's entourage. The Carter administration's admission of the shah to the United States on October 22, 1979 triggered a massive anti-American demonstration whose goal of attacking the US Embassy was averted. But on November 4, the anti-Bazargan government forces used the excuse of a meeting held in Algiers between Bazargan and Yazdi with then US National Security Adviser Zbigniew Brzezinski as a pretext finally to attack and occupy the embassy.

Khomeini's endorsement of the embassy seizure after the fact reflected both internal and external concerns. The creation of a faqih-ruled Islamic republic being his overriding goal, he calculated that his support of the students' action would ensure the realization of his vision. At the time, their action was emotionally popular and seemed to have a mass support base. Concerned with the Carter administration's antirevolutionary attitude and its scrambling to find a substitute

US surrogate for the shah's regime in the Persian Gulf, Khomeini was suspicious of every move Washington made in the realm of Gulf security and stability. These moves included Secretary of Defense Harold Brown's visit to the Middle East (February 9-19, 1979) which took place at the time of the revolutionary seizure of power and his unprecedented statement that the United States would itself defend its vital interests in Gulf oil supplies by military force "if appropriate." They also included the US negotiations with Oman, Somalia, and Kenya for military facilities, and the dispatch of the USS *Constellation* and several supporting warships to the Indian Ocean and Arabian Sea, as well as the strengthening of the small US naval force in the Gulf itself.[11]

Contrary to conventional wisdom, the kind of nationalist and realistic nonalignment policy that Bazargan had been pursuing did not disappear with his resignation in November 1979. Iran's foreign policy split down the middle between two major orientations. Both Abol Hasan Bani-Sadr, first as acting foreign minister and then as the first president of revolutionary Iran, and Sadeq Qotbzadeh, Iran's foreign minister, hewed to a foreign policy line that was close to the nationalist nonalignment policy of Mossadegh and Bazargan. Although Bani-Sadr rationalized his "equidistance" policy in Islamic terms, he would rely on Western Europe or France as a counterbalance to the superpowers.[12] Qotbzadeh, no less than his archrival Bani-Sadr, believed in a nonalignment policy, using the Mossadeghist term "negative equilibrium" with what he called "honesty in word and in deed."[13] They, therefore, like their predecessors—Mossadegh, Bazargan, Sanjabi, and Yazdi, who preferred the term positive neutralism—were all Iran firsters. And as such, they were all opposed by the revolutionary idealists who claimed to follow "the Imam Khomeini line" (*khat-e imam*) rather than "the Mossadegh path" (*rah-e Mossadegh*).

These idealists were the architects of the other major foreign policy orientation. They interpreted Khomeini's policy statements to suit their own predispositions and interests. Their interpretation involved, above all else, two major foreign policy issues: Iran's relations with the East and the West and Iran's export of the "Islamic Revolution." In his overriding concern with establishing a faqih-ruled Islamic republic, Khomeini said on December 9, 1979, "A nation that cries in unison that it wants the Islamic Republic, it wants neither East nor West but only an Islamic republic—this being so, we have no right to say that the nation that engaged in an uprising did so in order to have democracy. . . ."[14] This statement was made at the height of the Azarbayjan crisis over the adoption of the new constitution. Within this context, Khomeini was emphasizing that in engineering the new republic, Iran should not blindly imitate Eastern socialist or Western capitalist models, claiming that "Islamic democracy" is superior to both Eastern and Western democracies. The idealist interpretation has left out the key phrase "but only an Islamic republic" and has used the slogan "neither East nor West" to advocate that Iran should not have relations with either the Soviet or the US governments, nor with governments closely associated with the superpowers.

Regarding the other issue, Khomeini believed in the universal validity of Islam and its export to the rest of the world. In his words, Islam "is not peculiar to a country . . . even the Muslims. Islam comes for humanity . . . Islam wishes to bring all humanity under the umbrella of justice. . . ."[15] *"We hope this will gradually come about."*[16] As a corollary to this concept of an ideal Islamic world order, Iran, as the only faqih-ruled Islamic republic, "should try hard to export [its] revolution to the world."[17] But, he added emphatically, "It does not take sword to export this ideology. *The export of idea by force is not export.*"[18] In the same speech he added that the way to export revolution was by setting an example of Islamic ethical behavior. The idealists' interpretation overlooks the fact that the call to establish an Islamic world order is what Khomeini called an expression of hope. It prohibits the use of force and requires the export of the revolution through Islamic good behavior.

Two examples of the conflict between these contending foreign policy orientations during the hostage crisis would suffice. Bani-Sadr worked hard to transfer control of the hostages from their captors to the government so as to obtain their eventual release. He and Qotbzadeh supported the visit of a United Nations commission of inquiry to Iran for that purpose, but the students opposed it. Finally, when the commission was allowed to visit, even before its arrival in Tehran, Khomeini decreed that the hostage dispute would be settled by the Majlis, which was yet to be elected. At Bani-Sadr's urging, the Revolutionary Council recommended (by a vote of eight to three) the transfer of the hostages to government control, only to be rejected by Khomeini. He was supporting the students for the same reasons that he had initially endorsed the seizure of the US Embassy.

The other example relates to the export of the revolution. The students, in pursuing the export of the revolution and in defying the wishes of Foreign Minister Qotbzadeh, sponsored an international conference of some 16 national liberation movements from across the world. Other revolutionary idealists, such as Muhammad Montazeri, the late son of Ayatollah Hoseyn Ali Montazeri, took it upon themselves to try to export revolution by any means, including the use of force. He organized the Iranian Revolutionary Organization of the Masses of the Islamic Republic and wished to dispatch Islamic fighters to Lebanon as early as December 1979, long before the Revolutionary Guards were sent there in 1982. He was opposed by Bani-Sadr and Qotbzadeh just as he had been by Bazargan.

The settlement of the hostage dispute ended the students' control of Iran's US policy, a control that could not have been sustained for long without Khomeini's blessing. The stock interpretation that Iran finally decided to take the initiative on September 9, 1980 to settle the hostage dispute—because the hostages were no longer needed as a means of consolidation of power by Khomeini and his followers— requires reconsideration for three reasons. First, although *institutionally* power had been relatively consolidated—with the adoption of the constitution, the election of the first president, and the election of the first Majlis and its first speaker by September 1980—the ideological and political struggle between Bani-Sadr and his disparate supporters and the triumvirate of Muhammad Beheshti, Muhammad Ali Raja'i, and Hashemi-Rafsanjani and their unruly followers became more acute after Khomeini took the initiative to settle the dispute. Second, the US freezing of $12 billion in Iranian assets and varying degrees of economic sanctions by other Western nations exerted significant pressure on Iran. For months Bani-Sadr and the Central Bank believed that the freeze would not affect Iranian assets in US banks in Britain and the rest of Europe and resorted to litigation to try to free the assets, but their efforts were unsuccessful. Third, Iran feared an Iraqi invasion. Border skirmishes had escalated; Iran believed that Iraq's rapprochement with Saudi Arabia included some kind of military coalition. In addition the Soviet Union rejected all Iranian demands to cut off Soviet arms supplies to Iraq.

Far from ending Iran's confrontational foreign policy, the settlement of the hostage dispute actually intensified it. Believing that the increased activities of the United States in the Persian Gulf, beginning as early as February 1979, aimed at the containment and ultimate destruction of the revolutionary regime, the Iranians saw the United States as the real instigator of the Iraqi invasion of Iran on September 22, 1980. Paranoid or not, this view of the war as having been "imposed" by the US "deputy," Saddam Hussein, to use Montazeri's characterization, was in part responsible for the Iranian decision to carry the war into Iraqi territory in July 1982. The revolutionary idealists who suspected the United States of supporting Iraqi war efforts, and who dreamed of marching to Jerusalem through Karbala, won the debate of the day with the revolutionary realists who were skeptical. In the six-year interval between July 1982 and July 1988 when Iran accepted the UN-brokered cease-fire, the idealists' foreign policy orientation often prevailed over that of the realists.

Iran's confrontational foreign policy left it with only one major ally in the Middle East, and that was Syria.[19] All the other states of the region felt threatened in varying degrees by Iran's crusade to spread the revolution. In response to this perceived threat as well as that of the spread of the Iran-Iraq war to their territories, the six Arab Gulf states established the Gulf Cooperation Council in 1981 as a protective mechanism.[20] The export of the revolution by propaganda and annual demonstrations during the *hajj* in Saudi Arabia isolated Iran within the region, as did its dispatch of Revolutionary Guards to Lebanon and its support of the Lebanese Hizballah and Islamic Amal. It was further isolated by suspicions of its complicity in the attempted coup in Bahrain in 1981 as well as the suicide car bombings of US and French forces in Lebanon in October 1983 and acts of violence in Kuwait.[21] In addition, the holding of American, British, French, and German hostages in Lebanon by reputedly pro-Iranian groups was at

least encouraged in part by Iran's anti-Western, confrontational foreign policy, which further isolated it.

The crusade to export the revolution, furthermore, aggravated the
difficulties in Iran's relations with the Soviet Union. The ethnic and
geographic proximity of the two countries fueled the USSR's concern
about the possible contagion of the Islamic revolution among Soviet
Muslims. In a real sense, both the United States and the USSR wished
to contain Iran's destabilizing export of the Islamic revolution. To be
sure, the Soviet invasion of Afghanistan and especially the resumption
of Soviet arms supplies to Iraq in 1982 were the more influential factors in the troubled Soviet-Iranian relations, but Iran's campaign to
propagate its revolution was a major factor in Moscow's view of Iran's
"anti-Sovietism." Even the economic relations between the two countries were affected and did not improve until 1986, by which time
Iran's idealistic confrontational foreign policy had been significantly
tempered.[22]

Realistic Conciliation

The revolutionary idealists could not then, and do not now, care
about Iran's international isolation to which their confrontational foreign policy has so largely contributed. They repeatedly refer to one
of Ayatollah Khomeini's statements to support their foreign policy orientation: "We must become isolated in order to become independent."[23] But as Majlis Speaker Hashemi-Rafsanjani has since complained, such Khomeini statements are often quoted out of context.
This statement was made at the time of the hostage crisis when, in
fact, Iran had become internationally isolated partly because of Western diplomatic sanctions and partly because of the international disap-
probations voiced by the UN Security Council and the International
Court of Justice.

Just as Iran has had its revolutionary idealists since the beginning
of the revolution, it has also had revolutionary realists. They both believe that Islam is, and should be, the prime unit of people's loyalty
in the Iranian polity, but they sharply differ on the relative weight of

"Iranianness" and "Islamicness" in the Iranian identity. They also differ in their attitudes toward the existing international system. The idealists are world revolutionaries who want to establish an Islamic world order *now*, despite the fact that Khomeini said, "We hope this will gradually come about."[24] The realists, on the other hand, who also hope for an Islamic world order, are willing to come to terms with the realities of the existing international system. Hence, unlike the idealists, they are conciliatory in their foreign policy orientation. Khomeini referred to the differences between the two groups as "two schools of thought" and Hashemi-Rafsanjani calls them "factions." Whatever the label, the important cautionary point is that the fluidity of Iranian revolutionary politics is such that today's idealists may be tomorrow's realists and vice versa, and idealists on one set of issues may be realists on another. This is why the nature of revolutionary Iran's foreign policy is neither linear, nor dialectical, but *kaleidoscopic*.

As the supreme arbiter of Iranian affairs, Khomeini himself fit neither the idealist nor the realist categories. There were two major reasons for this. First, given the fluidity of Iranian factional politics, he looked after Iran's overall interests by performing the role of the balancer, throwing his weight behind one faction or another, depending on the circumstances. Second, his entire career as the leader of the Islamic opposition to the shah's regime and as the supreme leader of Iran from 1979 to 1989 revealed a complex mixture of idealism and realism in his leadership that was difficult for Westerners to comprehend, leading to such pejorative American journalistic labels as "fanatic" and to the constant surprise of the American body politic over the "disarray" of his foreign policy. He endorsed the taking of US hostages, and yet he released them. He decided to continue the war, and yet he finally ended it. Khomeini himself kept changing the Khomeini line.

Under one set of circumstances Khomeini contributed to Iran's international isolation and under another led the campaign to break that isolation down. Yet, all these actions aimed at the fundamental goal of Iran's independence under a faqih-ruled Islamic republic. The first requirement of Iran's independence, he said as early as December

1979, is what he called "intellectual independence," which required, among other things, that "we should learn the good things from foreigners and reject the bad things. . . ."[25] At the time, he held up the examples of Japan and India for Iran. On October 27, 1982, he said that Iran must end its hermit status in the world and, at his initiative and with his approval, President Ali Khamanei launched Iran's "open-door" foreign policy on July 30, and reiterated it on August 6, 1984—a policy that he said involved "rational, sound and healthy relations with all countries" and aimed at serving Iran's interest and ideology.[26]

Khomeini himself said on October 29, 1984 that it was "inadmissible to common sense and humanity" not to have relations with other governments "since it would mean defeat, annihilation and being buried right to the end. . . ."[27] Going even further, he said on November 2, 1985 that, "we do not want to live in a country which is isolated from the rest of the world. Today's Iran cannot be that way. Other countries cannot close their borders to others either; it would be irrational. Today the world is like one family, one city. In the present world circumstances we should not be isolated."[28] This is "the new thinking" in Iran; Hashemi-Rafsanjani calls it "interdependence."

What, then, does the conciliatory open-door foreign policy mean for the "neither East nor West" principle? It means that in pursuing its overriding goals of Islamic revolution and Iranian independence, Iran must reject both Eastern and Western domination of any kind. In his statement of October 3, 1988, Khomeini categorically announced that a deviation from that principle would be "treachery to Islam and the Muslims," without spelling out what that principle meant.[29] But Hashemi-Rafsanjani immediately added that it meant "loyalty to the goals of the Islamic Revolution, independence and negation of foreign domination."[30]

The idealists have rejected this realist interpretation of the principle. When Iran sent a low-ranking delegation to Leonid Brezhnev's funeral, for example, or when Iran's relations with the Soviet Union seemed to be improving, the radicals objected. As a result, the Foreign Ministry sent no one to Konstantin Chernenko's funeral, but in the latter case Foreign Minister Ali Akbar Vilayati said that the "objectives of the slogan ['neither East nor West'] is the negation of alien domination and not snapping of communication. . . . Nowadays, negating political relations with other countries means negating identity of the countries."[31] With respect to Iran's relations with the West, when the radicals objected to the expansion of Iran's relations with West Germany and even with Turkey, Hashemi-Rafsanjani said that world realities mean "we do not always have the power to choose. *I believe our principles are obeyed, but in some cases we may be limited and we may have to forego some of these principles.*"[32]

The issue of postwar reconstruction has intensified the debate between the idealists and the realists about the participation of foreign capital and technical know-how in the Iranian economy. While such leaders as Prime Minister Mir Hoseyn Musavi would seem to begrudge such participation, at least by some countries, others welcome it. Hashemi-Rafsanjani, for example, said on October 21, 1988 that "we should absorb skilled manpower from abroad and programs should be designed to encourage the return to Iran of skilled Iranians now residing abroad. . . ."[33] And Khamanei said on October 7, 1988 that when Iran faces shortages it "should use foreign resources. . . . We cannot prolong the issue of reconstruction for 100 years. . . ."[34]

And deeds speak louder than words. Even before the Iran-Iraq cease-fire, more than 70 percent of Iran's total imports came from Canada, Japan, and Western Europe, and more than 50 percent of its total exports went to these same areas.[35] While West Germany and Japan were the main exporters to Iran in 1987, the United States was Iran's main export market until the Reagan administration imposed a total ban on Iranian imports in the fall of the year.[36] Despite the increase in the total value of Iran's trade with the Soviet Union in that same year, it was only around $250 million as compared with about $2.5 billion with West Germany alone. Iran's economic relations with both the East and West are expected to expand in the postwar era.

Iran's principle of the export of the revolution is also undergoing change. The realists insist that the Islamic revolution must start at home, or in what they call the "Islamic citadel." Even Ayatollah Montazeri, reputedly yesterday's arch-supporter of the export of the revolution, today says that the way to export the revolution is to "build our country on the basis of Islam" so that it becomes "a model for other deprived countries."[37]

Again, deeds speak louder than words. Mehdi Hashemi, the chief activist exporter of the revolution, was arrested after his faction attempted to smuggle arms to Saudi Arabia during the hajj in 1986 and before his faction leaked the news of former US National Security Council Adviser Robert McFarlane's visit to Iran in conjunction with the US-Iran arms deal scandal. He was executed in 1987.[38] Since the acceptance of the cease-fire, the realists have helped with the release of seven French and German hostages in Lebanon, as of this writing, and the release of British hostages may be in the cards as well. Nine American hostages remain in captivity in Lebanon. Iranian leaders have repeatedly offered to help with their release, but it is unlikely that this can actually take place without an improvement in overall US-Iran relations. Iran may also try to distance itself from the Supreme Assembly of the Islamic Revolution in Iraq (SAIRI), which is linked to the Iraqi underground *al-Da'wa* dissidents, depending on the degree of progress made in the peace process. The opening of a SAIRI branch in Damascus may be a move in the direction of eventually moving its headquarters out of Iran.

More important to those observers who insist that Iran's continuation of the war after 1982 aimed at the export of the revolution, Khomeini's acceptance of UN Resolution 598 must suggest that at least for the Iranian realists the first priority is the building of the Islamic revolution at home rather than its export. Despite the reservation, if not outright opposition, of Interior Minister Ali Akbar Mohtashemi to Resolution 598, he at least implied in his statement to the Majlis on September 12, 1988 that after Khomeini's acceptance he was not opposed to the wishes of the "absolute imam." At least for the moment, the differences between the idealists and the realists on the question of war and peace appear to have been resolved in favor of the realists, who are in the political ascendancy.

Iran's decision to accept the cease-fire and to commit itself seriously to the peace process reflects an acute interplay between its battlefield setbacks and its deteriorating socioeconomic conditions. Until February 1987, Iranian leaders had repeatedly promised a "final victory," and once even specified a victory by March 21, 1987, the Iranian New Year. Although the Karbala-5 offensive threatened Basra and sent shockwaves throughout the Gulf and all the way to Washington, its failure—despite, or because of, the massive loss of life by the Revolutionary Guards—made Iran realize for the first time that the war could not be won. Hashemi-Rafsanjani frankly said: "To tell the truth, we cannot see a bright horizon now, so far as ending the war in its present form is concerned . . ."[39] He meant *winning* the war.

It was no coincidence, therefore, that in July 1987, for the first time, Iran did not reject a UN resolution out of hand, although admittedly Resolution 598 was more sensitive to Iran's position than the previous ones. Iran had quietly opted for a diplomatic solution to the war, probably some time after the effects of the disastrous Karbala-5 offensive sank into the consciousness of the Iranian leaders. No matter how important the subsequent battlefield setbacks at Faw Peninsula, the Majnun islands, and Shalamjah beginning in April 1988, the fact remains that Iran had already been involved in prolonged discussions with UN Secretary General Javier Perez de Cuellar long before the advent of these setbacks.

Even these military setbacks coupled with the Iraqi *al-Hussein* missile raids on Iranian cities between February 29 and April 18, 1988, however, would probably not have impelled Iran to opt for peace when it did had it not been for mounting economic hardship and the seemingly unbreachable deadlock on socioeconomic reforms. The widespread economic hardship caused by the war intensified in 1986-87 because of a dramatic drop in oil revenues, resulting from an unprecedented fall of oil prices in 1986 and an equally unprecedented increase in Iraq's capability for disrupting Iranian oil exports. The Iraqi attacks on Iranian oil shipments could reach as far south as the Iranian trans-shipment station on Sirri Island and even the terminal on Larak Island, farther south in the Strait of Hormuz. The US quasi-war with Iran made it possible for Iraq to disrupt Iran's oil exports with impunity.

The economic situation became so desperate that on November 13, 1987 the Iranian government called for a "financial jihad," urging those Iranians who could not fight in the war "such as women, the sick, and those with other excuses," to give financial support instead.[40] But as President Khamanei complained, the rich hung back and were not forthcoming. Khomeini lowered the boom on the rich with his decree of January 6, 1988. He tried to break the long-standing logjam on measures for social justice and economic betterment caused by the veto of government reform bills by conservative members of the Council of Guardians. He created a 13-member review council to oversee the decisions of the Guardians in "the interest of the Islamic country."[41] And in accepting the ceasefire in 1988 in a war that he could not win, Khomeini opted for the survival of the "Islamic Revolution," just as he settled the hostage dispute in 1981 for the same overriding purpose.

Twin Implications

This discussion began with 1978, the year that marked the culminating point in Iran of the rising twofold alienation from the shah's regime and from the United States. It will end with the central implications of Iran's kaleidoscopic foreign policy orientations for both countries during the first decade of the revolution. For Iran, there are two: The revolutionary regime needs to come to terms with the realities of the modern world and it needs to come to terms with itself.

The current debate between the revolutionary idealists and the revolutionary realists—like the earlier debate between the revolutionary nationalists and revolutionary Islamists on the nature of Iran's foreign policy—reveals the still unresolved underlying differences. Yet, the Iranian experience over the decade has produced new ideas that may point the way for Iran to come to terms with the modern world without sacrificing its Islamic ideals. Khomeini unequivocally stated what Iran's conception of the world should be if it is to come to terms with it: "Today the world is like one family, one city."[42] This is a conception that Hashemi-Rafsanjani calls an "interdependent world" and that prompted Khomeini to announce, "We do not want to live in a country which is isolated from the rest of the world."[43] The real challenge facing the revolutionary realists today lies in their persuading the revolutionary idealists to accept this conception as a foundation of Iran's foreign policy.

For most of the decade, the revolutionary idealists have, in effect, rejected this conception of the world, insisting on substituting their view of creating an Islamic world order by pursuing a confrontational foreign policy toward both the East and the West, accompanied by an aggressive crusade to export the Islamic revolution by propaganda rather than by setting a good example of Islamic behavior as Khomeini decreed. This policy has isolated Iran internationally to the detriment of its interests and its humane Islamic ideals.

Besides pointing out this lesson, the realists could demonstrate the inescapable reality of the diffusion of world culture, a culture marked by the advancement of science and technology and an insatiable quest for economic betterment, social justice, and political freedom that knows no international boundaries. Both revolutionary Russia and China tried to reject the concept of an interdependent world culture and both have ended up accepting it. They had no other choice; nor does revolutionary Iran.

The tension between the relative weight of "Islamicness" and "Iranianness" in the Iranian sense of national identity has continued ever since the Arab invasion of Iran in the seventh century. It has been intensified only in the context of an acute encounter between Iranian culture and world culture since the nineteenth century, and especially since the advent of the populist Iranian Revolution a decade ago. The well-known Iranian intellectual Jalal Al-e Ahmad prescribed that Iranians could best resolve this historical tension if the "modernized intellectuals" (*raushan-fekran*) could unite their political forces with those of the traditional *'ulama*. He did not live to see that in the Iranian Revolution, as in all previous instances of popular uprisings, the coalition between the two would prove to be ephemeral. To date, even the moderate religio-political Iran Liberation Movement of Bazargan, which is the only "loyal opposition" group in Iran, is not allowed to criticize government policies peacefully and freely. Even such a moderate opposition group charges it is subjected to acts of intimidation and violence.

For the United States, the implications of the Iranian Revolution suggest a need for America to come to terms with the fact that at least some of Iran's hostile words and deeds are a direct result of Washington's own misguided policies both before and since the revolution. In fact, as seen, the eruption of the revolution itself in part reflected alienation from the United States, most of all because of the popular perception that it was smothering Iran's sense of dignity and independence by its military, economic, and political support of the shah's regime almost to the very end of his repressive rule.

One would hope that the more conciliatory foreign policy emerging from Iran, combined with that of the administration of George Bush, might occasion a serious reassessment of America's Iran policy. Tehran and Washington might stop their mutual and destructive smear campaigns as a first step in the direction of a constructive and open dialogue. Even an implied approval of such a dialogue by Khomeini would have lent it the kind of legitimacy that the realists need, now that he is gone, to cope with the enormous challenge of what may be called the "twofold *perestroika*" of postwar reconstruction and social and economic reforms. To meet this challenge, the realists need to broaden and deepen their support base among the people. And to help that process along, the United States needs to place its relations with Iran during the second decade of the revolution on a plane of reciprocal interests and mutual respect.

NOTES

1. For the earliest characterization of the revolution in these terms, see R.K. Ramazani, "Iran's Revolution in Perspective," in American Foreign Policy Institute, *The Impact of the Iranian Events upon Persian Gulf and United States Security*, Washington, DC, 1979, pp. 19-37; Ramazani, "Iran's Foreign Policy: Perspectives and Projections," Joint Economic Committee of the United States Congress, *Economic Consequences of the Revolution in Iran* (Washington, DC: US Government Printing Office, 1980), pp. 65-97; and *Idem.*, "Iran's Revolution: Patterns, Problems and Prospects," *International Affairs* (London), Summer 1980, pp. 443-457.

2. See R.K. Ramazani, *The United States and Iran: The Patterns of Influence* (New York: Praeger, 1982).

3. In reality, however, the shah often used the US as its surrogate. See R.K. Ramazani, "Who Lost America: The Case of Iran," *The Middle East Journal*, vol. 36, no. 1 (Winter 1982), pp. 5-21.

4. See R.K. Ramazani, *The Foreign Policy of Iran, 1500-1941: A Developing Nation in World Affairs* (Charlottesville: University Press of Virginia, 1966), pp. 63-65.

5. See Akbar Hashemi-Rafsanjani, *Amir Kabir Ya Qahreman-e Mobarezeh Ba Iste'mar* (Amir Kabir or Champion of the Struggle against Colonialism) (Qom: Entesharat-e Farahani, 1346, [1967/8]).

6. For the original text of this important interview with *al-Dustur* in Arabic, see the December 24-30, 1979 issue or the translation in Foreign Broadcast Information Service, *Daily Reports*—Middle East & North Africa (FBIS-MEA), (Washington, DC), January 3, 1980, p. 25.

7. FBIS-MEA, March 13, 1979, p. R-10.

8. See Mohandes Mehdi Bazargan, *Enqelab-e Iran dar Dau Harekat* (The Iranian Revolution in Two Phases) (Tehran: Chap-e Sevom, 1362, [1983/84]), especially pp. 110-111.

9. For details, see R.K. Ramazani, "Treaty Relations: An Iranian-Soviet Case Study," in Albert Lepawsky, Edward H. Buehrig, and Harold D. Lasswell (eds.), *The Search for World Order* (New York: Appleton-Century-Crofts, 1979), pp. 298-311.

10. FBIS-MEA, March 13, 1979, p. R-11.

11. Although Washington geared up its muscle-flexing tactics on December 4, 1979, the Iranians had been watching US pressure tactics in the Gulf since February with increasing concern. Secretary Brown's visit to the Middle East and his statement were fully reported, for example, in *Ettela'at*, 1 Mordad 1358 (July 23, 1979), p. 12. Iran also put its Navy on alert around the Strait of Hormuz; see *Ettela'at*, 2 Mordad 1358 (July 24, 1979), p. 12. See also R.K. Ramazani, "The Genesis of the Carter Doctrine," in George S. Wise and Charles Issawi (eds.), *Middle East Perspectives* (Princeton: The Darwin Press, Inc., 1981), pp. 165-180.

12. See FBIS-MEA, November 21, 1979, p. R-9. Bani-Sadr believed that "despite the historical and ideological differences between the West and Iran, the two sides' interests were not so far apart." FBIS-MEA, November 20, 1979, p. R-30.

13. Besides "negative equilibrium," Qotbzadeh listed the other principles of Iran's foreign policy as follows: "non-interference in the affairs of other countries; a policy of an independent Iran; independence in decision-making; and harmonizing ideologies and politics." FBIS-MEA, December 21, 1979, p. 27.

14. FBIS-MEA, December 10, 1979, p. 29.

15. *Ibid.*, December 18, 1979, p. 10.

16. FBIS-South Asia (SA), February 11, 1987, p. I-2, (author's emphasis).

17. *Sourush* (Tehran), March 1981, pp. 4-5. For more details see R.K.

68 *Iran's Revolution*

Ramazani, "Khumayni's Islam in Iran's Foreign Policy," in Adeed Dawisha (ed.), *Islam in Foreign Policy* (Cambridge: Cambridge University Press, 1983), pp. 9-32.

18. Ramazani, "Khumayni's Islam," (author's emphasis).

19. For details, see R.K. Ramazani, *Revolutionary Iran: Challenge and Response in the Middle East* (Baltimore: The Johns Hopkins University Press, 1986; paperback, 1988), pp. 176-178.

20. See R.K. Ramazani, *The Gulf Cooperation Council: Record and Analysis* (Charlottesville: The University Press of Virginia, 1988).

21. See R.K. Ramazani, "Iran's Revolution and the Persian Gulf," *Current History*, January 1985, pp. 5-8, 40-41; *Idem.*, *Revolutionary Iran*, pp. 42-52, 175-195; and *Idem.*, "Socio-Political Change in the Gulf: A Climate for Terrorism?," in H. Richard Sindelar III and J.E. Peterson (eds.), *Crosscurrents in the Gulf: Arab and Global Interests* (New York: Routledge, 1988 for the Middle East Institute), pp. 127-151.

22. See R.K. Ramazani, "Iran," in Richard F. Staar (ed.), *Yearbook on International Communist Affairs*, 1987 and 1988 volumes, pp. 432-436 and 408-412 respectively.

23. *Gozaresh-e Seminar* (Tehran), no. 2, 1983/84, p. 36. Also see R.K. Ramazani, "Revolutionary Iran's Open Door Policy," *Harvard International Review*, January 1987, pp. 11-15.

24. FBIS-SA, February 11, 1987.

25. FBIS-MEA, December 14, 1979, p. 12.

26. FBIS-SA, July 31, 1984, p. I-2 and August 7, 1984, p. I-2.

27. *Ibid.*, October 30, 1984, p. I-1.

28. *Ibid.*, November 4, 1985, p. I-2.

29. For Khomeini's reconstruction guidelines, see FBIS-Near East & South Asia (NES), October 4, 1988, p. 46-48.

30. *Ibid.*

31. Staar, *Yearbook 1988*, pp. 408-412.

32. Emphasis added. FBIS-SA, April 17, 1987, p. I-3.

33. FBIS-NES, October 21, 1988, p. 43.

34. *Ibid.*, October 11, 1988, p. 59.

35. See R.K. Ramazani, "Iran: Burying the Hatchet," *Foreign Policy*, Fall 1985, pp. 52-74.

36. See the table in *Middle East Economic Digest*, August 12, 1988, p. 8.

37. FBIS-NES, October 31, 1988, p. 73.

38. See Ramazani, *Revolutionary Iran*, paperback edition with an epilogue on the US-Iran arms deal, pp. 253-269.

39. As quoted in the *Economist* (London), February 14, 1987, p. 30.

40. FBIS-NES, November 13, 1987, p. 61.

41. FBIS-NES, January 7, 1988, p. 50.

42. FBIS-SA, November 4, 1985, p. I-2.

43. *Ibid.*

Iran and
Western Europe

Anthony Parsons

Over a period of four centuries, the states of Western Europe had become accustomed to dealing with the Persian Empire. The ruling dynasties had changed from Safavid to Zand to Qajar to Pahlavi, but the structure of kingship provided the continuity. Shah Muhammad Reza Pahlavi's celebration of 2,500 years of uninterrupted monarchy in 1971 may have been an exercise in hyperbolic bombast but, in contemporary terms, Iran, to European observers, seemed likely to provide an exception to the 20th century Asian and African experience that, sooner or later, kings must give way to republican-minded colonels or radical politicians. By the mid-1970s, the shah had become part of the regional, indeed the global, landscape; he had reigned and ruled for more than 30 years. The kings of Egypt, Libya, Iraq, and Afghanistan had gone, and the Pahlavi court, with its aura of success and wealth, had become a magnet for deposed European monarchs: Greeks, Italians, and Albanians were among the frequent royal visitors.

Moreover, Pahlavi Iran had assumed increasing importance to Western Europe during the decades following the end of World War II. Iranian oil exports were never used as a political weapon as were Arab oil exports in 1956, 1967, and 1973. The oil nationalization crisis in 1951 had led to an apparently stable relationship between Iran and an Anglo-Dutch-American consortium. With the termination of British protection over the Arab states of the southern Gulf in 1971, Iran had, with Saudi Arabia, become a key player in the maintenance of regional stability and of the free flow of oil through the Strait of Hormuz.

Admittedly, in the turbulent aftermath of the 1973 Arab-Israeli war, the shah had been primarily responsible for the threefold increase in the price of crude oil from the Organization of Petroleum Exporting Countries (OPEC) and all that this meant in relation to the disruption of international finance, recession, and inflation. But the massive wealth that accrued to Iran from this transaction transformed the country into a highly lucrative export market and source of investment finance. Iran provided substantial loans to Britain and France and invested in West German industry. European industrialists, businessmen, and merchant bankers poured into Tehran in search of the vast contracts arising from the doubling, in 1974, of Iran's Five-Year Plan and the shah's determination to make Iran the Japan of the Middle East—the drive to be characterized as the Great Civilization. (It should be noted that it was the OPEC price hike that made economical the exploitation of British and Norwegian North Sea deposits. When OPEC's posted price was below $7 a barrel, North Sea development was not cost effective.)

Quite apart from its enhanced importance from the commercial and financial points of view, Iran had, by 1978, assumed wider significance for Western European foreign policy interests. The shah was using his country's wealth and influence to promote objectives that were complementary to those of the European Community—a "moderate" Arab approach to the Palestine problem, independence for Namibia, economic development in non-Marxist sub-Saharan Africa, Afghanistan, the Indian subcontinent, and other places. With the Soviet Union active in Angola, Mozambique, and the Horn of Africa, with a communist takeover in Afghanistan in 1978, and continued tension in the Arab Middle East, Iran came to be regarded as a weighty regional buttress to overall Western, not simply American, geopolitical interests. In short, Pahlavi Iran in the shah's last years was more attractive materially and more important politically to Western Europe than at any previous period in modern history, with the possible exception of World War II following the German invasion of the Soviet Union.

In 1978-79, the utterly unexpected happened. The apparently im-

pregnable monarchy, supported by a loyal officer corps and a pervasive secret police force (SAVAK), was brought down by cumulative
popular protest, giving birth to a regime that was in all respects the
antithesis of Pahlavism: republican austerity replaced imperial osten-
tation; America's second closest ally in the region became her sternest
adversary; a fierce independence of foreign entanglements replaced a
growing network of overseas connections; social and cultural Western-
ization gave way to fundamentalist Shi'i Islam. "Death to the Shah.
Neither East nor West. Only Islamic Republic." This slogan of the revolution said it all.

The member states of the European Community have spent the past
10 years trying to come to terms with this phenomenon and to protect
their interests as best they can in the profoundly changed circumstances. This article will set forth a balance sheet of their successes
and failures with special reference to Britain, France, West Germany,
and Italy.

Bilateral Relations

Britain

Of these four, Britain was the most dangerously exposed to hostile
reaction from the revolutionaries. Since 1953, the United States, previously regarded by Iranians as a potential St. George pitted against the
dragon of British imperialism, had itself become the super-dragon of
Iranian popular sentiment. America was seen as the destroyer of nationalist hero Muhammad Mossadegh, the principal abettor of an "illegitimate" shah, the corruptor of the Iranian-Islamic tradition through
the permeation of mass Western culture, the overwhelming presence
that Iran must shake off in order to be truly independent—in a phrase,
"the Great Satan."

Iranian folk memory is long, however, and Britain was still, to use
Ayatollah Ruhollah Khomeini's colorful characterization, "the aged
wolf of imperialism." Britain (and Tsarist Russia) had dominated Iran
from the early 19th century until 1918, and Britain had continued to

do so when the 1917 revolution removed Russia from the imperial stage. Britain had monopolized Iranian oil for half a century (until Mossadegh nationalized the Anglo-Iranian Oil Company in 1951) and, as Iranians saw it, had exploited Iran's natural wealth to its (Britain's) advantage. In Iranian mythology, Britain had been behind Reza Shah's seizure of power in the 1920s. Britain (and the Soviet Union) had invaded Iran in 1941 and had put Reza Shah's son on the throne. Britain's might had declined in relation to that of the United States, but the hidden British hand was still everywhere: Britain's scheming had manipulated the American juggernaut that had crushed Mossadegh; Britain was the shah's partner in the Central Treaty Organization (CENTO) which debarred Iran from its natural place in the Non-Aligned Movement. Britain, once the leader, was now second only to America in popular Iranian demonology, the Soviet Union occupying a different, although equally disagreeable area of the Inferno.

In the year of the revolution it became abundantly clear to observers that all Britain's efforts over the previous quarter century to bury the past and construct a normal relationship with Iran, free of paranoia and neuroses, had yet to bear fruit. From the shah downward, within the regime and among the opposition, the legend was ineradicable. Britain could not have changed its spots. If clever enough, one could always trace a British motive and British plotting behind all events, even those destructive of Pahlavi rule or, indeed, British interests.

France

France was less exposed. Defeat in the Napoleonic Wars had eliminated it from the competition for political and military influence in Iran during the age of imperialism; Britain and Tsarist Russia had scooped that pool. Throughout the 19th century, however, French cultural influence, as in Egypt, grew without posing the "imperialist" threat of the British and later the American equivalents. By the beginning of the 20th century, the Western-educated classes in Iran were Francophone rather than Anglophone. Iranian intellectual opponents of the shah at the time of the constitutional crisis of the early 1900s were operating from Paris rather than from London or St. Petersburg, and French political ideas were permeating Iranian intellectualism. By the 1970s, France had built a close relationship with the shah and his Paris-educated empress and with the Pahlavi establishment. French cultural and commercial interests were flourishing, but, at the time of the revolution, the pattern of the previous 80 years repeated itself. Harried by the authorities in his exile in southern Iraq, Ayatollah Khomeini flew to Paris where he was joined by leading Francophone supporters, notably Sadegh Qotbzadeh (later foreign minister and executed in 1981) and Abol Hasan Bani-Sadr (later president but forced to flee to Paris in 1981). The suburb of Neauphle-le Château became the headquarters of the revolution from which the ayatollah was free to issue his directives. Unlike the American and British embassies, no attacks were made on the French Embassy in Tehran, and France must have been hopeful that the revoltuion would leave French interests in Iran relatively unscathed.

West Germany and Italy

West Germany had even less to worry about. Except for the brief period of intimacy between Reza Shah and the Nazi regime, from the 1930s up to his enforced abdication in 1941, there was no history of special political or military relations between the two countries. In the post-World War II period, Germany concentrated with great success on promoting its commercial and industrial interests and steering clear of political entanglements. By the time of the revolution, Germany was by far the largest European exporter of goods and services to the Iranian market and was in the process of constructing two nuclear power stations at Bushehr on the Persian Gulf. German technology had penetrated the traditional manufacturing sectors of the urban bazaars, and thousands of Iranian workers had been trained in German factories. The German cultural center in Tehran (the Goethe Institute) had made itself available to opposition literary figures. Germans in Iran were liked and respected without resentment. Italy, too, had a promising commercial relationship. Italian engineers were active in dam building and an Italian firm was managing a huge urban development near Bandar Abbas in southern Iran.

Britain's Fate

For some months in 1979 the revolution took a predictable course. Alongside a formal government headed by Mehdi Bazargan, which was trying to reconcile popular aspirations with domestic tranquility and a realistic sense of national interest, an informal apparatus of power had come into existence, comprising Revolutionary Committees and the incipient Revolutionary Guard Corps. It soon became clear that these ardent spirits, confident of the ultimate backing of Ayatollah Khomeini, were outside the control of the constituted authorities. The saga of the Anglican Church, long established in Isfahan and other cities, was a case in point. The church was an obvious target, combining as it did an evangelical alternative to Islam and a historic connection in Iranian folklore with the British Embassy and the protection of the British government.

In February 1979, the pastor at Shiraz, an Iranian, was murdered. Between June and October, the Christian hospitals in Shiraz and Isfahan and the Mission for the Blind were confiscated; the bishop's house and diocesan offices in Isfahan were invaded and looted of documents and personal effects; the bishop, again an Iranian, was interrogated himself by a revolutionary judge. In October, an attempt was made on the bishop's life during which his wife was wounded. In May 1980, a female British missionary was savagely attacked in Tehran and the bishop's son was murdered. In August, five missionaries—including three British subjects, among them the woman who had been attacked—were arrested by local authorities. The three Britons were released in February 1981, following the intercession of Terry Waite, the Archbishop of Canterbury's envoy, shortly after the release of another detained British subject. By that time, all Anglican activities had been proscribed. At all stages the authorities had shown sympathy with the church's predicament, but had been powerless to act.[1]

Simultaneously, bilateral diplomatic relations between Britain and Iran declined to the lowest level ever, stopping short of a formal breach. In August 1980, a major demonstration took place outside the American Embassy in London at which about 80 Iranians were arrested. Some went on hunger strikes, and hunger-striking demonstrators organized a sit-in outside the British Embassy in Tehran. The British government wisely withdrew the staff in anticipation of their suffering a fate similar to that of their American colleagues, who at the time had been held hostage for nine months. Sweden was asked to look after British interests although the Iranian Embassy in London remained open. Shortly before this development the Iranian Embassy had been invaded by dissidents of ethnic Arab origin. The siege was broken by the British Special Air Service (SAS) who stormed the building and released the Iranian staff. From that time until December 1988, Britain was represented in Iran only by a small interests section under the Swedish flag. Following a bizarre incident in 1987, when a British diplomat in Tehran was abducted and beaten in retaliation for the arrest of an Iranian consular official in Manchester on a charge of shoplifting, all British staff were again withdrawn. In late 1988, agreement was reached to restore diplomatic representation, and a British chargé d'affaires was soon back in Tehran.

Assassins on the Seine

The tranquility of Franco-Iranian relations did not last. Paris again became the focal point for Iranian plotters, from radical republicans to liberal constitutionalists and extreme monarchists. In Paris in 1979, able and popular Prince Shahriyar Shafiq, son of Princess Ashraf, the shah's twin sister, was assassinated, presumably by agents of the regime. In 1980 an attempt was made on the life of the shah's last prime minister, Shapour Bakhtiar, in his Paris apartment. In February 1984, Paris was the scene of the assassination of General Ghulam Hoseyn-Ali Ovaisi, formerly commander land forces and martial law commander in 1978; Ovaisi had also been in Baghdad shortly before the Iraqi invasion of Iran in September 1980.

In 1981, the wide spectrum of Paris-based dissidents was joined by ex-president Bani-Sadr, along with Massoud Rajavi and other leaders of the radical Mujahidin-e Khalq who had been routed after fierce street battles in Tehran. They formed the National Resistance Council for Liberty and Independence with Rajavi at the head. The presence in France of these dissident groups soured relations between Paris and

Tehran. Bani-Sadr and his associates were granted political asylum on condition that they not engage in political activity; an Iranian demand for extradition was refused. There were anti-French demonstrations in Tehran—France was already unpopular because of its military aid to Iraq. Ambassadors were mutually withdrawn, and French nationals were advised to leave Iran.

In the years to come, France's progressively pro-Iraqi stance kept relations with Tehran at low ebb, compounding Iranian resentment at the Paris-based plotting. In 1984 a bomb exploded at the Tehran train station killing 18 people and injuring 300. Majlis Speaker Hujjat al-Islam Ali Akbar Hashemi-Rafsanjani blamed France for this outrage as the harborer of "criminal leaders." Simultaneously an Air France aircraft was hijacked to Tehran; the hijackers' demand for the release of those arrested for the 1980 attack on Bakhtiar was not met and the incident ended peacefully.

In 1986, the new French prime minister, Jacques Chirac, set out to normalize relations with Iran in the hope that Tehran would use its influence to bring about the release of two French journalists held hostage by Shi'i extremists in Beirut. A high-level French delegation visit to Tehran had preceded this initiative. A French line of credit was opened and the journalists were freed. Iranian anger at the presence of opposition activists was assuaged by the French expulsion in early 1987 of Mujahidin leaders (who then settled in Baghdad where they organized the National Liberation Army, which fought not entirely ineffectively on the Iraqi side).

The Franco-Iranian rapprochement was short-lived. In July 1987 the French judicial authorities wished to question an Iranian national named Vahid Gordji in connection with a series of murderous bomb attacks in France. Gordji claimed diplomatic immunity and took refuge in the Iranian Embassy. French police surrounded the building. The French Embassy in Tehran was reciprocally besieged, and a charge of drug smuggling and espionage was trumped up against a French diplomat. France severed relations.

It was not until the run-up to the French presidential elections in 1988 that the imaginative diplomacy of Prime Minister Chirac (now a candidate for the presidency) succeeded in mending the fences.

Gordji was allowed to leave France without interrogation; the siege of the French Embassy was lifted; France repaid the large loan borrowed from the shah for the subsequently cancelled nuclear power stations contract; and the remaining three French hostages in Beirut were released. Diplomatic relations were resumed.[2]

West Germany and Italy have experienced a less stormy passage than Britain and France, as might have been expected, and their commercial enterprises have continued to prosper. There have been minor incidents, however. In 1982, there were clashes between Iranian factions at Mainz and 17 were deported; Iran briefly closed its embassy and consulates. In 1983, Sadegh Tabatabai, a former senior government official, was arrested at Dusseldorf for allegedly smuggling opium. He was released on bail a few weeks later and returned to Iran. The Italians and Iranians had a short row over the showing of a television film derogatory to Khomeini and, in 1984, an Iran Air aircraft was hijacked to Rome, probably by Mujahidin. The hijackers later surrendered. These incidents, however, were no more serious than similar events in the days of the shah.

Following this brief sketch of bilateral relations, it is appropriate to look at how the two sides, Europe and Iran, fared in the major events that dominated the first decade of the revolution in the eyes of the outside world—the hostage crisis and the Iran-Iraq war.

The Hostage Crisis

If the Iranian leadership believed that the 14-month crisis, which began with the seizure of the American Embassy in Tehran in November 1979, could be isolated as an Iranian-American dispute, they were quickly disillusioned. The UN Security Council was concerned with the problem from the outset and the whole world—East, West, and nonaligned—reacted with horror to the outrage. Europe was no exception. Britain and France, the two European permanent members, gave the United States full support in the Council and voted for the sanctions resolution sponsored by the United States in January 1980 (vetoed by the Soviet Union, most probably as a result of the bad blood between the superpowers arising out of reaction to the Soviet invasion of Afghanistan a few weeks earlier). Meanwhile West Germany had already announced the suspension of credit guarantees to Iran. Britain had frozen all Government of Iran and Central Bank assets in London.

After the defeat of the sanctions resolution, the United States formally broke relations with Iran, applied an economic embargo and urged its European allies to do likewise. The European Community, to American annoyance, was reluctant to do so, not, as many Americans suspected, out of commercial greed but more because sanctions were regarded as probably counter-productive and conducive to strengthening the Iranian extremists and because of fear that a Western embargo would deliver the Iranian economy into the hands of the Soviet Union and its COMECON partners. Support in the Security Council had been given out of loyalty to an ally in distress, not out of a conviction that sanctions would accelerate the end of the crisis. Eventually the Community adopted a package of sanctions that was more symbolic than actual. An embargo on exports to Iran was adopted, but it applied only to contracts concluded prior to November 4, 1979 (and in the case of Britain only those concluded after June 1980). There was also dissent between the United States and the Community over the legitimacy of the freezing of Iranian assets in the European branches of American banks.

By the end of the summer of 1980, when war with Iraq was clearly threatening and the Iranian leadership was beginning to realize that there was nothing further to be gained from a prolongation of the hostage crisis, the fact that West Germany had maintained good relations with the new regime proved a valuable asset. Sadegh Tabatabai made contact with the German ambassador in Tehran, whom he knew well, and sought his mediation to meet with US representatives. This contact was arranged through the auspices of Bonn and proved to be the first move in the process of negotiations that led eventually to the release of the hostages.[3]

In retrospect, in spite of occasional American irritation with its allies, the United States had no cause for complaint at the solidarity shown by Europe. More important perhaps for the future, Tehran should have concluded that gross infringements of international behavior were likely to be met with a monolithic response from the West and that there was no serious chance of dividing the United States from her partners—the bizarre and cynical behavior of the United States and of certain European governments in regard to horse (or arms) trading for the release of hostages held by Iranian backed Shi'i gangs in Beirut lay far in the future.

The Iran-Iraq War

When Iraq invaded Iran on September 22, 1980, the UN Security Council did not even meet for several days. Iraq, wanting no international interference with what President Saddam Hussein, perhaps acting on the advice of the same Iranians whose counsel had proved so disastrous to the shah, wrongly believed to be a short blitzkrieg, brought strong and successful pressure on the seven nonaligned members of the Council to oppose a meeting; none of the rest of the membership, including the Europeans, was disposed to override this obstacle. The continuing hostage crisis had alienated international opinion to the extent that no state was ready to come to Iran's defense. By the same token, the Europeans supported the first resolution (No. 479 of September 28) which, while calling for a cessation of hostilities, did not demand Iraqi withdrawal from Iranian territory. Even after the hostage crisis ended in January 1981, the Council maintained its pro-Iraqi bias.

By 1982, Iraq was very much on the defensive and clamorously ready for peace; Iran was perceived internationally as obstinately prolonging the war by insisting on its original war aims of "identifying and punishing the aggressor." The Europeans supported all the resolutions that called for withdrawal to internationally recognized frontiers when it was a question of Iran withdrawing from Iraqi-occupied territory, and went along with the tendency of the Council to address its strictures to both sides even when it was clear that it had been Iraq which had, for example, initiated the "tanker war," air attacks on open cities, and the use of poison gas. In only one statement by the president of the Council, in March 1986, was Iraq specifically cited for the use of chemical weapons. Interestingly, in 1987 and 1988, membership in the Council included all four of the European states under discussion—Britain and France (permanent members) as well as West Germany and Italy (non-permanent members). They were all active in the formulation of Resolution 598 on which the present peace talks are based.

Bilateral European attitudes toward the war differed somewhat from the solidarity demonstrated in the Security Council. From the outset, Britain adopted a policy of strict neutrality, embargoing the export of all military equipment to both sides except for the ill-defined category of "non-lethal" items. This proviso enabled Britain to export to Iran a large supply ship originally contracted to the shah's government, and the Iranian Purchasing Office, a center in London for the acquisition of weaponry on the international private market, remained open until 1987. Britain also dispatched a small force of warships, the Armilla Patrol, to the southern Gulf in 1980 to render assistance to British merchant shipping.

France, on the other hand, came down openly on the Iraqi side in 1981 with the supply of Mirage F-1 aircraft (which Iran described as an act of war). Simultaneously France, under strong Iranian pressure, agreed to release to Iran three missile launching boats that had been ordered by the shah (of which one was briefly hijacked in the Mediterranean by the former commander in chief of the Imperial Iranian Navy). In 1983, the French foreign minister visited Baghdad, and France subsequently loaned to Iraq five Super-Etendard aircraft armed with Exocet missiles. There is no doubt that these acquisitions made a significant difference to Iraq's capability, particularly in the "tanker war" and attacks against oil installations on the Iranian side of the Gulf. France, with the United States, was also one of the most vociferous advocates of a unilateral arms embargo against Iran when Tehran equivocated over Resolution 598; Britain was almost equally enthusiastic.

Germany and Italy, with major interests in both camps, pursued a neutral policy throughout the war. Italy, however, joined other European governments—Britain, France, Holland, and Belgium—in sending warships to the Gulf in 1987 when the foreign armada gathered there to escort flag-shipping, thus inhibiting Iranian retaliation and giving greater impunity to the Iraqis to prosecute their campaign against Iranian shipping and oil installations.

When, on July 18, 1988, Iran, to the astonishment of the world and probably its own people, announced its acceptance of Resolution 598, international opinion began to turn away from its long-held pro-Iraqi posture. The threat of an outright Iranian victory, with its profound consequences for the region as a whole, had disappeared, and, for a few weeks, Iraq appeared for the first time as the recalcitrant party. In particular, Iraqi use of chemical weapons against military and civilian targets, unequivocally cited in reports by a UN mission, excited strong censure and led to the unanimous adoption of Security Council Resolution 620 on August 26, 1988. This resolution, cosponsored by West Germany, Italy, Britain, and Japan (but not France), called for consideration of appropriate measures should there be any further use of chemical weapons, wherever and by whomever. It was followed on September 15 by an overwhelming vote of censure by the European Parliament, accusing Iraq of using chemical weapons in Kurdistan and calling on the European Community governments to suspend the sale of arms and "chemical substances and equipment" to Iraq.

Europe has returned to a more impartial position between Iran and Iraq and, following the autumn 1988 negotiations between London and Tehran, all Community governments now have or are about to have full diplomatic relations with Iran. The wheel has come close to full circle after ten years. The only major imbalance that remains is the total absence of relations between Iran and the United States.

Interstate Economic Relations

The fluctuations in the fortunes of material interests are a useful barometer of interstate relations. Conventional wisdom insists that there is a major political ingredient in commercial relations between industrialized and Third World countries, in particular where the latter tend toward socialism or corporatism and the government has a major say in the award of large contracts. The oil-rich states of the Middle East are often cited as prime examples of this theory. There was certainly some truth in this notion in the days of the shah. Although the majority of "bread-and-butter" trade in the private sector was done on the basis of commercial norms—prices, delivery dates, and after sales service—there is no question that political (and other less reputable) factors entered into the award of public-sector contracts—for such projects as power stations, steel mills, nuclear reactors, military equipment, roads, railways, and ports. All other things being equal, a particular country could expect to benefit from a close political relationship and vice versa. In this context it is useful to examine the performance of the six principal Organization of Economic Co-Operation and Development (OECD) countries (West Germany, Japan, France, Italy, Britain, and the United States) over the decade since the revolution. The following is a comparative table showing the position in 1978 and in 1987:

TABLE 1

OECD Percentage of Iranian Import Market

	1978	1987
Germany	21.9	26.2
Japan	17.4	17.5
Italy	6.9	8.4
Britain	9.4	8.3
France	5.8	3.0
United States	23.9	.9
	85.3	64.3

Certain interesting deductions can be drawn from this table. First, the decline in the OECD Six share in the total market has fallen by 21 percent, almost exactly by the amount of the decline in the US share of 23 percent. Second, the greater part of this gap has been filled by Turkey and Eastern European states such as Bulgaria and Yugoslavia which are conveniently situated to use the overland route to Iran via Turkey. Third, the European Community share has, notwithstanding the earthquake of the Iranian Revolution, remained almost constant: 44 percent in 1978, 45 percent in 1987. Fourth, Britain's share, in spite of the virtual absence of diplomatic representation, has remained stable; Iran was still among Britain's top 20 markets in the developing world in 1986 and, in the Middle East, third only to Saudi Arabia and the United Arab Emirates.[4]

Economists will assert that it is facile to draw firm conclusions from such statistics. But they suggest that even a violent and disruptive political event such as the Iranian Revolution does not necessarily change traditional patterns of trade except in extreme circumstances—such as the Iranian-US breach with its attending embargoes and freezing of assets among other factors. What will be really interesting to watch will be the impact of the inevitable return of US competition in the Iranian market, the absence of which led to a nearly 25 percent gap, quickly filled by others.

Conclusion

It is always perilous to attempt to gaze into the future, particularly when Iran is a factor. One important change, as far as Iraq-Iran relations are concerned, will be the departure of West Germany and Italy from the Security Council upon completion of their two-year terms as non-permanent members, thus weakening the Community voice in that forum which plays a crucial role in continuing the peace negotiations.

Provided that there is no recurrence of hostilities with Iraq and provided that there is no domestic upheaval in Iran which blows the leadership off its present course of mending fences with the outside world, provided the government abandons attempts to export the revolution and concentrates on domestic consolidation and economic reconstruction, there is even reason to hope that relations between Iran and the Community will move into quieter waters with advantagtes to both sides. So long as the breach with the United States remains open, Europe will figure prominently in Iranian calculations.

There are still problems to be solved. Europe expects Iran to use its undoubted influence to bring an end to the nightmare of the hostages held in Beirut. All the French and German hostages are now free but, apart from the Americans and others, there are still four British hostages in captivity. (A British subject has been held prisoner in Tehran for more than three years without charge or trial. Trumped up accusations of espionage have been leveled at him.) Until such problems have all been satisfactorily resolved, it is impossible to envisage a fully normal British relationship with Tehran.

In broader terms, the revolutionary leadership must realize that adherence to the accepted norms of international behavior is an essential precondition to the acceptance of Iran as a member in good standing of the international community. In these respects, the ball is in Iran's court. Europe, in turn, must recognize, as it seems to, that the revolution is a fact; there must be no backward glances over the shoulder or encouragement of plotters. Iranian affairs are for Iranians, not outsiders, to settle.

NOTES

1. For the incident involving the Anglican Church in Isfahan, see Bishop H.B. Dehgani-Tafti, *The Hard Awakening* (London: Triangle Books, 1981).

2. For information on Franco-Iranian relations, see *Middle East International* (London), Nos. 294 (February 20, 1987), 304 (July 11, 1987), 305 (July 25, 1987).

3. On the hostage crisis, see Warren Christopher et al. (eds.), *American Hostages in Iran: The Conduct of a Crisis* (New Haven, CT: Yale University Press, 1985). A Council on Foreign Relations Publication.

4. The 1978 and 1987 publications of the Committee for Middle East Trade (33 Bury Street, London) are a good source for Iranian trade statistics.

Soviet-Iranian Relations in the Post-Revolution Period

Shireen T. Hunter

At the time of the Islamic revolution of 1979, relations between Iran and the Soviet Union had reached a state of equilibrium. During the two previous decades, Iran had pursued a dual policy toward the Soviets—containing radical, often Soviet-supported, forces and pursuing economic cooperation with Moscow. The Soviet Union followed a similar policy toward Iran—emphasizing economic ties and at the same time supporting internal and regional forces that arose in opposition to the shah.

Since the 1979 revolution, the official guiding principle of Iran's foreign policy has been "Neither East nor West, only the Islamic Republic." In practice, however, this principle has not translated into equal treatment of the two superpowers and their allies; Iran's relations with the United States and the West have suffered more than its relations with the Soviet Union. The relatively closer Soviet-Iranian ties in the postrevolution period reflect the unique character of the Soviet-Iranian relationship, a uniqueness derived from the geographical proximity and overwhelming military superiority of the Soviet Union. Because of these factors, Iran simply cannot afford to overly antagonize the Soviet Union or to cut all communications with it. Even in times of crisis, Iran has not broken diplomatic relations with the Soviet Union as it has with Western powers such as the United Kingdom, France, and West Germany.

During the past decade, Iran's relations with the Soviet Union have developed erratically, fluctuating between periods of measured hostility and limited cooperation. These relations have been affected by Iran's factional rivalries, Soviet occupation of Afghanistan, tensions between Iran and both the East and the West, Soviet foreign policy priorities, and Soviet assessment of the balance of risk and opportunity in Iran and in the Middle East in terms of acquiring influence. As of this writing, prospects for dramatically improved Soviet-Iranian relations remain promising but by no means certain.

Expectations and Apprehension: 1979-1981

Immediately after the revolution, during the premiership of Mehdi Bazargan from February to November 1979, Soviet-Iranian relations did not change significantly. Bazargan's political philosophy owed much to former prime minister Muhammad Mossadegh's theory of negative equilibrium. As such, he was committed to an essentially non-aligned foreign policy for Iran and the maintenance of friendly, or at least reasonable, ties with all states, particularly Iran's neighbors. Thus, Bazargan recognized the need for Iran to accommodate the Soviet Union. As an Iranian nationalist, however, he also remained deeply suspicious of Soviet intentions.

Increased Soviet meddling in Afghanistan following the communist coup d'état of April 1978, Soviet insistence on the validity of Articles V and VI of the 1921 Soviet-Iranian treaty (which under certain circumstances allowed Soviet military intervention in Iran), suspicions regarding the Soviet role in Iran's ethnic troubles, and fear of Soviet-Iraqi collusion in the Arab agitation in Khuzistan all intensified Iran's apprehensions and excluded a significant improvement in Soviet-Iranian ties. On the other hand, at this time certain changes in Iran's foreign policy coincided with the aims of the Soviets. These changes included Iran's withdrawal from the Central Treaty Organization, the severing of its ties with Israel and South Africa, and its establishment of better relations with Syria, Libya, and the Palestine Liberation Organization.

In general, the Soviet Union viewed the Iranian Revolution with a mixture of apprehension and expectation. The Soviets hoped that the revolution would be transformed into a true socialist revolution.[1] At the same time, they worried that the revolution would lead to turmoil in Iran, which could then be used by the United States to justify military intervention and the establishment of a docile, pro-American regime. The Soviets also suspected Bazargan and his colleagues of pro-American sympathies. They found it hard to believe that the United States had "let the shah go" without ensuring that the successor regime would be equally responsive to its interests. Soviet suspicions were enhanced by events such as the meetings between Iran's Foreign Minister Ibrahim Yazdi and US Secretary of State Cyrus Vance in October 1979 and between Bazargan and US President Jimmy Carter's National Security Advisor Zbigniew Brzezinski in Algiers in November of 1979. Thus, the Soviets welcomed the fall of the Bazargan government following the seizure of the US embassy in Tehran on November 4, 1979.[2] The principal benefit for Moscow, as expressed by the leader of Iran's pro-Moscow Tudeh Party, was that as long as the crisis continued there would be no chance of normalization of US-Iranian relations.[3] Bazargan's fall also raised Soviet hopes for an eventual transformation of the Iranian Revolution into a socialist one.[4]

No immediate and dramatic improvement in Soviet-Iranian relations followed the fall of the Bazargan government. This situation is partly explained by the fact that Abol Hasan Bani-Sadr, who was elected to the presidency in January 1980, and Sadegh Qotbzadeh, minister of foreign affairs, were essentially Iranian nationalists and deeply suspicious of Soviet intentions.[5] These fears were exacerbated after the Soviet invasion of Afghanistan in December 1979, which many Iranians viewed as a first step in a Soviet thrust toward Iran and the Persian Gulf. The Iranian government condemned the invasion and withdrew from the 1980 Moscow Olympics. Nevertheless, economic necessities, created by the Western economic embargo of Iran in retaliation for the seizure of the American hostages, led to expanded Soviet-Iranian economic and trade relations. In April 1980, Iran's minister of economy and finance visited Moscow and signed a number of agreements on transit, trade, and other subjects.

Rapprochement: 1981-1983

By June 1981, with the flight from Iran of Bani-Sadr and the execution of Foreign Minister Qotbzadeh, radical Islamic factions had won the battle for control of the Iranian government. These factions, virulently anti-Western and anti-American, viewed the Soviet Union more benignly than had the previous regime and favored close Soviet-Iranian ties.

The Soviet Union and its supporters in Iran—especially the Tudeh Party, which had supported religious factions against Bani-Sadr—proceeded to form a tacit alliance with the radical wing of the Islamic faction. As a result, when the new Islamic leadership began a systematic elimination of leftist forces in 1982, the Tudeh Party was allowed to continue to operate. The strategy of the Tudeh Party and of the Soviet Union of supporting religious factions in their fight against the non-Tudeh left seems to have been based on a fear that a non-Tudeh leftist government in Iran would eliminate the Tudeh's chances of gaining power and would also be much less responsive to Moscow's interests. The Soviets and the Tudeh also seem to have concluded that a frontal attack on Islamic forces at this point would be counterproductive. Thus they opted for a strategy of gradual penetration of the Iranian bureaucracy and the military, which might enable them to seize power at an opportune moment.[6]

The Iran-Iraq War

In the early months of the Iran-Iraq war, between September 1980 and March 1982, the Soviet Union sided with Iran. It stopped sending supplies to Iraq and offered them to Iran. In addition to its longstanding desire to ingratiate itself with Iran, the Soviet attitude toward the war was determined by two factors:

■ Iraq, while still a Soviet ally and militarily dependent on Moscow, had been growing increasingly independent and was trying to distance itself from the Soviets to pursue its own regional ambitions.[7] Iraq had expanded its Western ties and, as early as 1977, had initiated contacts with the United States with the purpose of normalizing relations. The Soviet Union apparently felt that potential gains in Iran outweighed possible losses in Iraq.

■ In general the Soviet Union favored neither drastic shifts in the regional balance of power nor territorial changes on its border that it could not promote or control. Early in the war, Iraq seemed to be the country threatening the territorial and power equation in the region. As a result, the Soviet Union felt that Iraq should be contained.

The combination of these factors led to an appreciable Soviet-Iranian rapprochement. Soviet-made arms reached Iran indirectly and, according to some sources, Soviet advisers became involved in training Iran's Revolutionary Guard Corps and in organizing the country's intelligence services.[8] Trade also expanded, especially after the destruction of Iran's principal non-oil port in Khorramshahr increased the nation's dependence on transit trade through the Soviet Union. But even at the height of the Soviet-Iranian rapprochement, cooperation between the two countries remained limited. For example, Iran refused direct Soviet arms deliveries, and the issue of Iranian gas exports to the Soviet Union—which were interrupted after the revolution because of price disputes—remained unresolved.

Soviet-Iranian relations reached a turning point in the spring of 1982, when Iran—despite its military disarray—succeeded in forcing the withdrawal of Iraqi troops from its territory. At this point, the Soviets expected Iran to make peace with Iraq. Indeed, the Tudeh Party called for a cease-fire and peace negotiations. When Iran refused to negotiate and opted to seek military victory, the Soviet Union resumed shipment of military supplies to Iraq. Soviet leaders apparently concluded that an Iranian military victory would pose the greatest threat to the region's territorial and power equation and therefore had to be prevented.

Soviet Occupation of Afghanistan

A principal impediment to closer Soviet-Iranian relations in this period remained the Soviet occupation of Afghanistan. Even during the ascendancy of the pro-Soviet radical faction, the Iranian government continued to condemn the Soviet move. Failure to voice condemnation would have damaged Iran's Islamic credentials and undermined its claim to the leadership of the Muslim world. Moreover, the less extremist elements of the regime resisted the pressure for closer relations with the Soviet Union and used the continued Soviet occupation of Afghanistan as an argument against such relations. Later, the lifting of the Western economic embargo, the resumption of Iran's oil exports, and its adjustment to the loss of Khorramshahr reduced Iran's economic need for the Soviet Union, further slowing their rapprochement.

Of greater importance, by late 1982 the Soviets had reassessed the Iranian Revolution and the Islamic regime. Initially, Soviet theoreticians, commenting on the Iranian Revolution, had emphasized Islam's progressive potential. Following Lenin's thinking that at a certain stage of economic and political development, religion, like nationalism, can play a progressive role in the transformation of a society and can pave the way for a socialist transformation, the Soviets concluded that Islam could play a positive role in the Middle East.[9] Thus, many Soviet theoreticians viewed the religious factions in Iran as more progressive than such figures as Bazargan or Bani-Sadr, whom they characterized as bourgeois nationalists. It also seems that the principal criterion used by the Soviets for judging the degree of progressiveness of Iran's factions was the extent of their anti-Americanism. This assessment partly explains their preference for the anti-Western religious factions. The Soviets gradually discovered, however, that anti-Americanism did not automatically translate into pro-Sovietism.[10] This was particularly true of the less extreme religious elements or, in Soviet parlance, the reactionary clergy. The Soviets also began to view Iran's Islamic revolutionary ideology more as a competitor than as an ally, not only in the Islamic world but in their own Asiatic republics as well.

The Soviets were also beginning to reassess the impact of Iran's revolution in the Persian Gulf region and on their own prospects for influence in the area. Initially, they had hoped that the revolution would eliminate the US presence from the Gulf and would open opportunities for the expansion of Moscow's influence. By 1982, however, this had not happened. The Gulf Arab states had drawn closer together within the framework of the Gulf Cooperation Council. Because of their apprehension of the effects of Iran's Islamic revolution, they had also strengthened their ties to the United States. In other words, in terms of Soviet prospects for influence in the Gulf, the Iranian Revolution had the opposite effect of what the Soviets expected.

Fluctuation Between Conflict and Conciliation:
1983-1988

By the end of 1982, factors that had tended to bring Iran and the Soviet Union closer together had undergone considerable change, thus causing strains in their relationship. A major crisis in Soviet-Iranian relations occurred in April 1983 when Iran expelled 18 Soviet diplomats on charges of spying. Apparently information about the activities of Soviet diplomats in Iran had been passed on to Iranian authorities by the British government. The British, in turn, had obtained this information from a former Soviet vice consul in Tehran, a senior KGB official who had defected to Britain. He had also disclosed the extensive penetration of Iranian revolutionary organizations, bureaucracy, and the military by Tudeh members and Soviet agents. These revelations alerted Iranian authorities to the seriousness of a potential Soviet threat to their power base and led to extensive purges, including the ouster of the commander of the Iranian navy and of a special assistant to the speaker of the parliament.[11]

In the wake of these revelations, the Tudeh Party was banned and its leaders arrested and tried. Unlike other occasions, when it had overlooked the harsh treatment of communist parties in Middle Eastern countries, the Soviet Union reacted sharply to the treatment of the Tudeh. Soviet commentators, in both print and broadcasts, attacked the Iranian government.[12] Also, both directly and through such intermediaries as Syria and Libya, the Soviets warned Iranian authorities against the execution of Tudeh leaders. This warning was effective, and the life of Tudeh leader Nureddin Kianuri was spared. In retaliation for the Iranian crackdown on Tudeh, the Soviets withdrew their

experts from a number of important power plants and industrial installations under the pretext that Iraqi bombings had made working
conditions unsafe. They stopped short, however, of interrupting trade
and transit relations. In fact, even at the height of the crisis neither
country was willing to risk closing all doors of communication. In addition to the traditional factors that make Soviet-Iranian relations
unique, the Iran-Iraq war, US-Iranian hostility, and the situation in
the Persian Gulf militated against Iran's overly antagonizing the Soviet
Union.

The year 1983 also marked an erosion of the radicals' position and
the gradual emergence of a more moderate and pragmatic faction
within the Iranian leadership. This development would have considerable impact on the conduct of Iran's foreign policy, including the republic's ties with the Soviet Union. The crisis in Soviet-Iranian relations was defused in early 1984 when developments in the Persian
Gulf led Iran to seek a limited rapprochement. These developments
included increasing Iraqi attacks on Gulf shipping; US and Western
statements that they would not allow closure of the Strait of Hormuz;
the delivery of Stinger anti-aircraft missiles to Saudi Arabia; and, finally, the shooting down of an Iranian F-5 aircraft by Saudi Arabian
F-14 planes in June 1984. Iran and the Soviet Union both feared that
the United States would use the Persian Gulf crisis to justify military
intervention in the region. Their rapprochement aimed to deter US intervention.

In June 1984, the director general of the Iranian Foreign Ministry,
Muhammad Reza Sadr, visited Moscow and met with Soviet Foreign
Minister Andrei Gromyko. At the end of Sadr's visit, the two countries
issued a communiqué in which they expressed their opposition to foreign intervention in the Persian Gulf.[13] This meeting was followed by
a number of low- and middle-level visits to Iran by Soviet energy officials, and agreements were reached to resume work on a number of
development projects.

The rapprochement, however, was limited. For most of 1984 and
1985-86, despite periodic efforts at cooperation, Soviet-Iranian relations remained seriously strained. They would begin to improve only

after the outbreak of the Iran-contra affair in November 1986 and the US reflagging of Kuwaiti tankers in the summer of 1987.

In 1984, as the balance of power within the Iranian leadership began to shift in favor of the more moderate factions, Iran began a sustained effort to reduce its international isolation through active diplomacy and by emphasizing bilateral relations. One outcome of this change was an improvement in Iran's relations with the West. In July 1984, West Germany's foreign minister, Hans-Dietrich Genscher, visited Tehran. After his visit, he indicated that Iran might be willing to open up to the West.[14] In July 1985, the speaker of the parliament, Ali Akbar Hashemi-Rafsanjani, visited China and Japan. Iran's activist and pragmatic diplomatic strategy improved its international position and increased its economic and military options, including access to new sources of military supplies, thus reducing its dependence on the Soviet Union. It was also in this period that the secret US-Iranian contacts were made.

As stated previously, the Soviet Union had taken an increasingly pro-Iraq position since 1983. This decision, it seems, was not an easy one for the Soviet leadership to make.[15] The Soviet perception of greater opportunities for improving their position and status among the Arab states had finally tipped the balance against Iran. The new Soviet policy met with considerable, albeit limited, success. In 1985 the Soviet Union established diplomatic ties with Oman and the United Arab Emirates, followed by Qatar in August 1988, but Moscow failed to establish diplomatic ties with Saudi Arabia or to reduce US influence with the Arab states.

More numerous and effective Iraqi air strikes on Iran's civilian targets, largely with Soviet-made missiles, undermined the Soviets' popular image in Iran. Iranian officials, particularly those opposed to close Soviet-Iranian ties, used these Iraqi attacks as examples of Soviet animosity toward Iran.[16] Soviet commentators, for their part, attacked Iran's unwillingness to agree to a negotiated peace, Iran's intransigence on the Afghanistan issue, and Iranian assistance to some Afghan rebel groups.[17] The Soviet Union was also unhappy about Iran's working relations with such Western allies as Pakistan and Turkey.

Yet both sides exercised caution and kept relations from deteriorating beyond a critical point. For example, the Soviet Union, despite US complaints, did not prevent its East European, Arab, or other allies from providing Iran with certain types of weaponry. Iran, meanwhile, tightly controlled the Afghan groups operating inside its territory.[18] There were also periodic efforts at reconciliation and cooperation. In February 1986, Soviet First Deputy Foreign Minister Georgi Kornienko visited Tehran. Agreements on economic and commercial issues were reached, and the joint Soviet-Iranian Economic Commission was reactivated.

In the spring and summer of 1986, because of increasingly effective Iraqi bombings of Iran's oil installations and the Saudi policy of depressing oil prices, Iran's economic conditions severely deteriorated. To cope with these difficulties, Iran enlisted Soviet cooperation in efforts to shore up oil prices, and Iran also tried to resume the export of gas to the Soviets. As a gesture of good will, the Soviet Union agreed to reduce its oil exports by 100,000 barrels per day, but it did not respond to Iran's desire to resume gas exports, hoping to use that concession as a bargaining chip in the future.

Impact of the Iran-contra Affair

A significant breakthrough in Soviet-Iranian relations occurred in early 1987 following the revelations in November 1986 of the secret US-Iranian arms deal and the repercussions of the Iran-contra affair in Iran and in the United States. In Tehran, these revelations—plus the disclosure of the role played by Israel in the arms scandal—weakened the moderates' position and offered the radicals an opportunity to question their revolutionary credentials, to undermine their influence, to enhance their own positions, and to heighten anti-American feeling. Yet, for nearly two months the moderates tried to salvage the dialogue with the United States, and there was no immediate rush to improve ties with the Soviet Union. On the contrary, in a now-famous speech at Tehran University in November 1986, Foreign Minister Ali Akbar Velayati said that "Iran will never accept Soviet domination."[19] *Izve-*

stia responded by expressing surprise that such a comment should come from "an Iranian official in whom such lofty powers in the foreign policy field are vested."[20] More than Iran's internal political dynamics, the changes in US policy toward the Persian Gulf and the Iran-Iraq war prompted Soviet-Iranian rapprochement.

Prior to 1987, the United States tried to accomplish seemingly contradictory objectives in its Persian Gulf policy: (1) to contain Iran, prevent Iraq's collapse, and protect Gulf Arab states; (2) to keep the door open for future reconciliation with Iran—hence the ill-fated efforts of 1985–86. One consequence of the Iran-contra affair was a shift in US policy to active support of Iraq; the United States, therefore, did not respond to Iran's effort to salvage something of their dialogue. As a result, the pace of Soviet-Iranian rapprochement accelerated; the number of official visits between Tehran and Moscow increased, culminating in Velayati's visit to Moscow in February of 1987.

The 1987 US decision to respond to Kuwait's request to reflag 11 of its tankers, and the ensuing buildup of Western navies in the Persian Gulf, alarmed Moscow and Tehran. Iran feared a US military strike against its oil installations and worried that the United States might use its military presence to topple the Islamic regime. The Soviet Union both shared these fears and manipulated them to enhance its position in Iran, but its policy of seeking influence in both Iran and the Arab world and its continued military support for Iraq limited the scope of Soviet advances toward Iran. For example, the Soviet lease of three tankers to Kuwait led to an Iranian speedboat attack on a Soviet ship, the *Korateyev*, on May 6, 1987. This attack also seems to have been in retaliation for the Soviet military assistance to Iraq, which had increased since the Iranian capture of Faw Peninsula in February 1986.

The Soviets, however, reacted mildly to these events, and Soviet-Iranian reconciliation continued. By June 1987, the pace of Soviet-Iranian contacts accelerated, and in mid-June Soviet Deputy Foreign Minister Yuli Vorontsov visited Tehran. On this and other occasions, the two sides expressed their common view on the situation in the Gulf and called for the withdrawal of all foreign navies from the area. In the course of these contacts, the two sides also signed a number of agreements pertaining to transport of Iranian oil through Soviet territory, construction of a trans-Iranian railroad, joint exploration for oil in the Caspian Sea, and dam-building and industrial projects.[21]

During the summer and fall of 1987, Soviet-Iranian relations remained good. The Soviet Union supported some of Iran's conditions for acceptance of the UN Security Council's Resolution 598 by suggesting that there be a simultaneous cease-fire and the formation of an impartial committee to investigate responsibility for the start of the war. The Soviet Union also effectively prevented the imposition of a UN-sponsored arms embargo on Iran despite US efforts to impose it. None of these efforts, however, led to spectacular improvements in Soviet ties with Iran. Even the US-Iranian military encounter in October 1987—after an American-flagged Kuwaiti tanker, the *Sea Isle City*, was hit by a Silkworm missile—did not change this situation. The Soviet response to the US military attack on the Iranian oilfield at Rashadat was mild, illustrating that, although the Soviet Union was eager to enhance its position in Iran, it had no intention of sacrificing its other diplomatic goals in Europe and the United States.

In March 1988, Soviet-Iranian relations deteriorated further when Iraq began massive bombing of Iranian cities with modified Soviet Scud-B missiles. The Soviet Union denied that it had helped Iraq extend the range of the missiles, but Iranian Majlis Speaker Hashemi-Rafsanjani nonetheless accused the Soviet Union of pursuing a policy of "hypocrisy and duplicity." Even *Kayhan*, the Tehran daily, expressed dismay that the Soviet Union had not "taken stock of the advantages and gains of having the most anti-American country in the world for a neighbor" and complained that it had not shown its gratitude to Iran.[22]

A second factor was the Iranian moderates, never in favor of a tight embrace of the Soviets, who after their setback in 1987 had recouped some of their lost influence. Third, despite the skirmishes of October 1987, the US reflagging operations had not had a dramatic impact on the course of the war, and Iran's worst fears of the consequences of the US military presence had not materialized.

Finally, Iran's Soviet connection had not deterred the United States from sending its navy to the Persian Gulf. This factor became even more important after the US-Iranian military encounter of April 1988, when the United States destroyed a third of the Iranian navy, and when, on July 3, 1988, the USS *Vincennes* downed an Iran Air passenger plane. On both occasions, the Soviet official responses were mild, reflecting the priority its leaders attached to other foreign policy goals.

Relations after the Cease-fire

After a yearlong resistance, on July 18, 1988 Iran accepted Resolution 598 and agreed to a cease-fire to be followed by peace negotiations. Immediately after the cease-fire, the Soviet Union offered to organize direct talks between Iran and Iraq, but Iran refused the offer and opted for UN mediation. The Soviet Union continued its conciliatory approach, and during a visit to Tehran in November 1988, Soviet Deputy Foreign Minister Vorontsov admitted that "mistakes had been made in the last decade" and expressed the Soviet wish to make up for these mistakes and to help Iran in its reconstruction effort.[23] Iran, for its part, seemed interested in improving relations with Moscow, particularly in the fields of economics and trade. The Soviet Union took part in the Tehran trade fair in October 1988, and Iran held a trade exhibition in Moscow at the same time.[24] There was increased talk of expanding trade and economic relations.

For nearly six months, however, progress in Soviet-Iranian relations was slow. A combination of factors that in the past had prevented dramatic advances in a Soviet-Iranian rapprochement once again slowed the process of reconciliation. First, the political mood in Iran after the cease-fire was that of self-criticism and introspection. This criticism was particularly focused on the destructive consequences of Iran's unrealistic approach and the need for greater pragmatism and moderation. One result of this self-evaluation was the enhancement of the position of the moderates, although the radicals continued their resistance and opposition to their policies. Nevertheless, even this relative improvement in the moderates' position affected Iran's foreign policy, directing it more toward normalization and improvement of relations with Western countries.[25]

As of early 1989, however, this twin process of domestic and foreign moderation had stalled for several reasons. The radicals still wielded enough influence to resist efforts to substantially change the direction of Iran's policies. Also stalling the process were actions by the moderates who may have gone too far in criticizing the revolution and emphasizing its mistakes. This course seems to have provided the radicals with ammunition, supporting their warnings to Ayatollah Ruhollah Khomeini that this trend could endanger the very foundations of the revolution. Khomeini's inherent preference for equilibrium between the two factions led him to boost the radicals' influence. As a result, progress on relations with the West was stalled and prospects for better Soviet-Iranian ties were improved. The Soviets may also have played a role here. While official Radio Moscow broadcasts commented positively on Iran's efforts to improve its Western ties, Radio Moscow's "Peace and Progress" Persian broadcasts attacked efforts to normalize Iran's relations with the United States.[26] Another factor damaging the moderates' position was that Iran's pro-West policy did not pay the expected dividends—either in terms of support for the full application of Resolution 598, criticism of Iraq for the use of chemical weapons, or financial pay-offs in regard to favorable terms of credit.

Meanwhile, the Soviet Union's decision to withdraw its forces from Afghanistan made it easier for Iran to improve ties with Moscow. Consequently, beginning in December 1988, official Soviet and Iranian media commentary about each other became increasingly positive. For example, in an interview with *al-Hawadith*, Yuri Vinogradov, the Soviet special envoy to the Middle East, clearly stated that Iraq was obstructing the signing of a peace agreement by insisting that the 1975 Algiers agreement be considered invalid.[27] Radio Moscow commented that, given its size, population, economic power, and influence with Muslims, Iran should play an important role in resolving the Near East conflict.[28] Meanwhile, during a visit to Cuba in January 1989, Iran's Deputy Foreign Minister Muhammad Javad Larijani praised Soviet leader Mikhail Gorbachev, and especially his speech at the United Nations, which he said "made a superb impression." He added that with the end of the Iran-Iraq war and the Soviet withdrawal from Afghanistan, he saw "no obstacles" to the development of Soviet-Iranian relations. He also said that Iran supported basic Soviet goals in Af-

ghanistan after withdrawal.[29] An important event in the evolving Soviet-Iranian relations was the meeting of Ayatollah Khomeini's special representative, Ayatollah Abdullah Javadi Amoli, with Gorbachev on January 5, 1989. In a letter to Gorbachev, Khomeini reportedly called on him to study the Quran and said that "materialism cannot save humanity from the crisis of disbelief in spirituality." But he also expressed his joy that the Soviet government had recently allowed some mosques that had been closed for decades to operate freely.[30] Meanwhile, there were increased contacts between Iran (and the Iran-based Afghan rebels) and the Soviet Union regarding the future of Afghanistan. In January Soviet Deputy Foreign Minister Vorontsov visited Tehran and met with the eight Afghan groups.[31]

Impact of the Rushdie Affair

In February, Soviet-Iranian relations received another boost from an unexpected source: the controversy over Salman Rushdie's book *The Satanic Verses*. The radicals manipulated the Rushdie affair to discredit Iran's policy of opening to the West. Given the meager results of Iran's pro-West policy, their arguments about the futility of trying to improve relations fell on fertile ground. This development gave the visit of Soviet Foreign Minister Eduard Shevardnadze to Iran in February 1989 a special importance. In the course of his meeting with Shevardnadze (and a meeting with Khomeini was a rare occurrence in itself), Khomeini called for better relations. President Ali Khamenei asked the Soviet Union to pressure Iraq into withdrawing its troops from Iranian territory.[32] After the Shevardnadze visit, there was speculation about a Soviet-Iranian agreement on delivery of Soviet arms to Iran in a possible exchange for the delivery of Iranian natural gas. The Soviet Union came under attack from the United States and the West for exploiting the Rushdie affair for its own interest. Although the Soviets offered to serve as mediator in this controversy between Iran and the West, they refused to attack Ayatollah Khomeini's call for Rushdie's execution.

Despite dramatic changes in the atmosphere of Soviet-Iranian relations, part of the Soviet commentary on Iran remained highly negative.

Soviet criticism of Iran centered on the repressive nature of the regime, its human rights abuses, the mistreatment of leftist forces (particularly the Tudeh Party), and the general failure of the revolution to meet the population's expectations.[33] This Soviet attitude, however, is not surprising. It in fact reflects the Soviet Union's traditional pattern of behavior and is a variant of its two-track policy toward Iran.

Conclusion

Iran's relations with the Soviet Union in the postrevolution period have been affected by geopolitical and historical factors that have stemmed both from longstanding traditions and from the more recent effects of the revolution. The enduring importance of these factors has meant that Soviet-Iranian relations have retained their unique characteristics. Meanwhile, so far, the same factors have both argued against outright confrontation and excluded extremely close cooperation. For the Soviet Union, Iran has remained of particular interest, yet, as in the past, the Soviet Union as a superpower has balanced its interest in Iran with its other regional and global priorities. Thus it has determined its policy toward Iran on the basis of a cost-benefit analysis. Of the new factors the most important have been Iran's as yet unresolved power struggle, changes in Soviet Third World policy under Gorbachev toward a more risk-averting strategy, Iran's problems with the West, and regional conflicts such as the Iran-Iraq war and the Soviet occupation of Afghanistan. Of these factors, Western, especially US, policy toward the Persian Gulf region and the Iran-Iraq war has played a particularly significant role in Soviet-Iranian relations.

It appears that these factors will continue to affect Soviet-Iranian relations. Thus, the future of these relations will depend to a great extent on the evolution of the domestic political scene both in Iran and in the Soviet Union. For example, if the radicals continue to prevail in Iran, the chances for expanded and more cooperative Soviet-Iranian relations will improve.

Similarly, if with domestic reforms and the abandonment of its expansionist goals the Soviet Union becomes a more appealing partner, the likelihood of close Soviet-Iranian relations—even in the case of the victory of the moderates—will sharply increase. The extent of the Soviet-Iranian rapprochement will also depend on the attitude of Western countries toward Iran, especially on issues of special interest to it, such as the implementation of Resolution 598 and the settlement of the Shatt al-Arab problem. A lack of Western even-handedness on these issues would increase Iran's incentives for better ties with Moscow.

NOTES

1. For a more detailed discussion of these points see Shireen T. Hunter, *Iran and the World: Continuity in a Revolutionary Decade* (Bloomington, IN: Indiana University Press, forthcoming 1990), chapter 4.

2. There is no hard evidence pointing to Soviet involvement in the conception and implementation of the US Embassy takeover. It is interesting to note, however, that the mastermind of hostage operations, Hujjat al-Islam Khoeiniha, is widely known in Iran as "Moscow's man" and is an ardent and virulently anti-American advocate of close Soviet-Iranian relations. Prior to the revolution, he was known to have served as liaison between the Tudeh Party and the religious opposition.

3. See Eric Rouleau's interview with Tudeh leader Nureddin Kianuri in *Le Monde*, April 18, 1980, p. 5.

4. See Aryeh Yodfat, *The Soviet Union and Revolutionary Iran* (New York: St. Martin's Press, 1989), pp. 65-66.

5. For Bani-Sadr's comments on Soviet motives see interview in *Le Quotidien du peuple*, September 19, 1978, as quoted in Ali-Reza Nobari, ed., *Iran Erupts* (Stanford, CA: Iran-America Documentation Group, Stanford University, 1978), p. 283.

6. See "Red Plot Sparks Off Anti-Russian Frenzy," *Sunday Times* (London), May 8, 1983, p. 18.

7. Since 1979, Iraq had been trying systematically to become the dominant power not only in the Persian Gulf but throughout the Middle East. Part of Iraq's strategy was to convince Persian Gulf states that it was moving away from the Soviet Union and no longer posed a threat to them. Baghdad hoped that its efforts would lead Gulf states to loosen their ties with Western nations.

8. See Shahram Chubin, "Gains for Soviet Policy in the Middle East," *International Security*, vol. 6, no. 4 (Spring 1982), pp. 122-152.

9. See Leonid Medvedko, "Islam and Liberation Revolution," *New Times*, no. 43 (October 1979), pp. 18-21.

10. Soviet-Middle East analyst Alexander Bovin, for example, noted that the struggle "against the Western devil" appeared together with "a struggle against the Eastern devil." Quoted in Yodfat, *The Soviet Union and Revolutionary Iran*, p. 94.

11. See "Iran Tries Ex-Navy Chief," *Washington Post*, December 7, 1983, p. A-22, and "Iran Executes 10 Communists," *Washington Post*, February 26, 1984, p. A-25.

12. See V. Komarov, "Reign of Terror Against Patriots," *New Times*, May 21, 1983, pp. 10-11.

13. See "Gromyko and Iranian Meet on U.S. Moves in Gulf," *New York Times*, June 9, 1984, p. 5.

14. On Genscher visit, see Foreign Broadcast Information Service (FBIS), *Daily Reports*, Near East and South Asia (NES), July 24, 1984, p. I-2.

15. See Dennis Ross, "Soviet Views Towards the Gulf War," *Orbis*, Fall 1984, pp. 437-447.

16. FBIS-NES, March 21, 1988, p. 1.

17. See, for example, an *Izvestia* article on the subject of Iranian assistance to Afghan rebels, FBIS-Soviet Union (SOV), December 3, 1986, p. H-1.

18. In addition, Iran reacted mildly to Soviet and Afghan transgressions of its air space. Some reports have also alleged that Iran allowed the Soviets to set up a listening station in Baluchistan. See *Time*, March 8, 1982, p. 32.

19. For Velayati's speech see FBIS-South Asia, November 26, 1986, p. 11.

20. See "Izvestia Views Speech by Iran's Velayati," FBIS-SOV, December 9, 1986, p. H-1.

21. See "Iran and Soviets Draft Big Projects Including Pipelines and Railroad," *New York Times*, August 5, 1987, pp. 12-13.

22. For Hashemi-Rafsanjani's remarks see FBIS-NES, March 25, 1988, p. 2; for the Kayhan commentary, see *ibid.*, July 13, 1988, pp. 54–55.

23. See "Moscow Wants Role in Reconstruction," *Middle East Economic Digest* (MEED), vol. 32, November 25, 1988, p. 19.

24. See "Iranian Trade Exhibition Comes to Moscow," FBIS-SOV, October 13, 1988, p. 19.

25. During summer and fall 1988 and winter 1989, Iran resumed diplomatic relations with France, Canada, and Britain; there were also a number of high-level visits by Italian, German, and French officials to Tehran.

26. See "Iranian-U.S. Diplomatic Relations Discussed," FBIS-SOV, February 3, 1989, p. 29.

27. See "Foreign Affairs Official on MidEast Policy," *al-Hawadith*, reprinted in FBIS-SOV, January 31, 1989, p. 33.

28. See "Moscow Comments on Iran's Regional Policy," FBIS-SOV, December 1, 1988, p. 20.

29. For Larijani's comments see "Iran Welcomes Soviet Policy, Will Aid Pullout," FBIS-SOV, January 19, 1989, p. 25.

30. See "Khomeini Aides Meet with Gorbachev," *Washington Post*, January 5, 1989, p. A-27.

31. See "Tehran Talks, Visit Reviewed," FBIS-SOV, January 4, 1989, p. 22.

Also "Vorontsov Concludes 'Constructive' Talks in Tehran," FBIS-SOV, February 7, 1989, p. 32.

32. On Shevardnadze's visit see "Shevardnadze Meets Iran's Rafsanjani, Musavi," FBIS-SOV, February 28, 1989, pp. 25-26, and "Shevardnadze, Khomeini Meet in Tehran," *Washington Post*, February 27, 1989, p. A-1.

33. See "Correspondent on Iran's 'Shi'ite Dictatorship'," FBIS-SOV, December 1, 1988, p. 21.

Trial by Error

REFLECTIONS ON THE IRAN-IRAQ WAR

Gary Sick

In law, what plea so tainted and corrupt
But, being season'd with a gracious voice,
Obscures the show of evil? In religion,
What damned error, but some sober brow
Will bless it and approve it with a text,
Hiding the grossness with fair ornament?
—Shakespeare, *Merchant of Venice*

On September 22, 1980, the government of Iraq launched simultaneous strikes against all Iranian airfields within reach of its bombers,
while its massed armies advanced along a 450-mile front into Iran's
Khuzistan Province. On August 20, 1988, one month short of the
war's eighth anniversary, the guns fell silent after the government of
Iran, with great reluctance and after a full year of equivocation, accepted a United Nations cease-fire proposal—an act which the Ayatollah Ruhollah Khomeini characterized as "more deadly than taking
poison." After eight years of brutal conflict, the forces of these two
bitterly hostile foes ended the fighting very close to where they had
begun. Neither side achieved its war aims.

A cease-fire, of course, is not peace, and a genuine peace agreement
may not be achieved for a very long time. Consequently, it is still too
early to draw any final judgments about this war. The cessation of hostilities does, however, present an opportunity to reflect on the eight

years of this conflict and its lessons for the region and for the international community.

Both parties have portrayed the war as a noble crusade: Iraq as a historic defense of Arab sovereignty and rights against the marauding Persians; Iran as a holy war against the Baathist infidels. It is perhaps more instructive to regard this war as a colossal series of accumulated errors and miscalculations on the part of virtually all parties who touched or were touched by the conflict. What follows is not a history of the war; rather, it is one observer's account of several key turning points of the war, each involving major errors of judgment or execution by one or more parties.

The 1975 Algiers Agreement

Reduced to its essentials, the Iran-Iraq war was a dispute about borders, specifically a disagreement about the division of the waters of the Shatt al-Arab River—the confluence of the Tigris and Euphrates rivers—which separates the two countries in the south.[1] Although control of the river was a matter of contention going back to Ottoman times and beyond, the modern dividing line between the two independent states was first established in a border treaty in 1937. It provided for Iraq to control the river up to the bank on the Iranian side—with the exception of an eight-kilometer stretch before Abadan where the *thalweg* principle (centerline of the navigable channel) would apply. (Reza Shah reportedly later told his son that he regarded this as an error in judgment and regretted his acceptance.) In 1969, after the Baath Party assumed power in Baghdad, Iran unilaterally renounced the 1937 treaty and systematically began to challenge Iraqi control of the Shatt al-Arab by not flying the Iraqi flag on its ships and by refusing Iraqi pilots.

The issue appeared to be resolved in 1975, when Muhammad Reza Shah Pahlavi met with then Vice President Saddam Hussein of Iraq on the margins of the meeting of the Organization of Petroleum Exporting Countries (OPEC) in Algiers and surprised the world—and even their close friends and advisers—by adopting the thalweg as the dividing line along the entire river boundary. For several years previously, the shah, together with Israel and the United States, had supported a Kurdish insurrection in northern Iraq. In return for acceptance of the thalweg, the shah agreed to terminate support for the Kurds. This he promptly proceeded to do, dealing the *coup de grâce* to the Kurdish resistance. Observance of the treaty provisions by both Iran and Iraq was satisfactory from 1975 until the revolutionary takeover in Iran in February 1979. At that time, however, Iran still occupied several small pockets of land that were to be ceded to Iraq under the treaty.

Origins of the War: Iran

In the exuberant atmosphere following the overthrow of the shah, Iranian leaders displayed no interest in diplomatic niceties, much less support for any legacies of the shah's rule. Although Iran did not formally renounce the 1975 treaty, neither did it offer assurances that the treaty would be observed.[2] On the contrary, revolutionary leaders almost casually let it be known that they did not consider themselves bound by any of the shah's agreements. Instead, they pointedly noted that in traditional Islam there were no borders dividing the faithful. Those remarks, when coupled with fiery rhetoric calling for export of the revolution to all of the Islamic world, gave Iraq and other neighbors of Iran justifiable grounds for concern.[3]

From the beginning, Iran's hostility to the Iraqi regime had, in addition to its general revolutionary and ideological zeal, a personal edge to it. Khomeini had spent 13 years of his exile in the holy city of Najaf in Iraq, and he was well acquainted with the concerns of the Shi'i population and with the secular nature of Baathist rule. Khomeini was unceremoniously ejected from Iraq in October 1978 in response to the shah's complaints about his political activities, and the ayatollah viewed this as evidence of Saddam Hussein's sympathy with his arch enemy. Revolutionary Iran ignored Iraq's early efforts to develop satisfactory relations, and Iranian leaders made no secret of their support for the Shi'i opposition in Iraq.

Despite this, there were no major incidents between the two countries during the first year of the revolution. The situation began to deteriorate sharply in early 1980 when the Iraqi government arrested Ayatollah Muhammad Baqir al-Sadr, an internationally respected Shi'i clergyman. In early April 1980, bombs exploded at several locations in Iraq and there were attempts on the lives of two Iraqi officials, Tariq Aziz and Latif Nasif Jasim (who were later to become foreign minister and information minister respectively). Iraq suspected, probably rightly, that these events were the work of pro-Iranian opposition forces. Shortly thereafter, Ayatollah Baqir al-Sadr and his sister were reported to have been executed in prison by the Iraqis, setting off emotional shock waves in Shi'i circles in Iran and elsewhere.

In retrospect, it is evident that the events of April 1980 represented the crucial turning point that eventually led to war. Curiously, there is no evidence that either party protested interference in its domestic affairs by the other, although such activity was clearly prohibited by the 1975 treaty. Moreover, Iran, which was absorbed in its own revolutionary politics, seems to have ignored the danger signs and made no effort to reconstitute its military forces. On the contrary, as a result of repeated purges, Iran's military was in a state of almost total disarray.

Thus, Iran's behavior in the immediate post-revolutionary period left it with the worst of all possible worlds. Its rhetoric and meddling with the Shi'i opposition in Iraq was highly provocative, while its military weakness made it a tempting target. The combination proved deadly.

Origins of the War: Iraq

Iraq has claimed that its invasion of Iran on September 22, 1980, was carried out in self-defense, citing the well-known formula of the *Caroline* case in international law—that there was "a necessity of self-defence, instant, overwhelming, leaving no choice of means and no moment of deliberations."[4] The reality appears otherwise.

Iraq claims that Iranian aircraft violated Iraqi air space on 69 occasions between April and September 1980 and that on September 4 Iranian artillery opened fire across the Iraqi border from the three small parcels of land that were supposed to be returned to Iraq under the 1975 treaty. Assuming the accuracy of these charges, the subsequent Iraqi attack, which bombed targets throughout Iran and captured more than 4,000 square miles of Iran's Khuzistan Province, would appear to be disproportionate to the provocation. Iraq never claimed that Iran was massing forces, and the total absence of any Iranian military preparation was unmistakably obvious in the first few weeks of the war.

The available evidence suggests that Iraq conducted a systematic buildup of its military forces between April and September 1980 in preparation for a lightning offensive. On September 7, Iraq sent its first warning note to Iran and simultaneously sent troops to capture one of the disputed parcels of land. Other disputed areas were reclaimed in successive days, so that by September 13 the Iraqi chief of staff could declare that, "we have regained all the land areas which have been trespassed upon by the Iranian side and have settled our dispute with Iran concerning the land differences."[5]

Four days later, in a speech to the nation, President Saddam Hussein announced that, "Since the rulers of Iran have violated this accord . . . I here announce before you that the Accord of March 6, 1975 is terminated on our part too. Therefore, the legal relationship in the Shatt al-Arab must return as it had been prior to March 6, 1975."[6] He also renounced any claim on Iranian territory. In succeeding days, Iraq reported incidents along the river in the vicinity of Basra, and on September 22 its forces attacked.

Given this sequence of events, Iraq's claims of urgent self-defense are less than totally convincing. Observers in the region and elsewhere interpreted these claims as a diplomatic fig leaf to justify an attempt to overthrow a revolutionary regime in Iran that posed a serious threat to Iraqi internal stability. Iraqi thinking seems to have been based on the following elements:

■ A belief that the Iranian military was so disorganized and demoralized in the wake of the revolution that it would no longer be capable of resisting a determined military attack;

■ Interest in altering the terms of the 1975 Iran-Iraq border agreement to reestablish Iraqi sovereignty over the Shatt al-Arab, as well as regaining Arab control over the southern Gulf islands of Abu Musa and the Tunbs that Iran had occupied in 1971;

■ Longstanding Iraqi claims on Khuzistan (which Iraq officially described as "Arabistan") and an apparent conviction that the Arab population of that territory would welcome "liberation" by Iraq;

■ Apparent belief (probably reinforced by Iranian exiles and opposition elements) that Khomeini's rule would be unable to survive what was expected to be a lightning military defeat and that a successor regime would be composed of individuals less hostile to the existing order;

■ Expectation that a quick and total defeat of Iran would shift the balance of power in the Persian Gulf, fulfilling Iraq's ambition to be regarded as a regional superpower and as a leader in Arab politics.

Ironically, the results of the Iraqi invasion produced a set of results precisely the opposite of those intended. The attack helped Khomeini to consolidate his control by rallying nationalist sentiments around the revolution, suppressing internal critics, and accelerating efforts to rebuild an effective military machine along Islamic lines. The Arab population of Khuzistan resisted the Iraqi advance. Iraq's military offensive stalled by November 1980 as Iranian resistance stiffened. As Iran began to counterattack effectively, slowly driving Iraqi forces back toward the border, Iraq's great gamble was widely perceived as a failure, undermining its regional influence and leaving it far more dependent on the financial and political support of its oil-rich Arab neighbors than ever before.

The UN Security Council: 1980

Just as Iran and Iraq blundered into war, the United Nations stumbled badly in its initial efforts to halt the conflict. During the first six years of the Iran-Iraq war, most of the actions of the Security Council varied between leaving things much as they were or making them worse.

The Security Council first met to discuss the war on September 26, 1980, four days after Iraq launched its attack. On September 28 the Council adopted Resolution 479 calling for a cease-fire. This resolution was notable on two accounts. First, it referred to the conflict as a "situation" rather than a "war," thereby evading the Security Council's responsibility under the UN Charter to determine if an aggression had occurred; and second, it called for no withdrawal of Iraqi forces, which by then had penetrated well into Iran's Khuzistan Province.[7] When both parties ignored it, the Council put the subject aside on October 24 and did not raise it again for nearly two years.

The Council's lackadaisical approach to its responsibilities on issues of international peace and security was more than oversight. Iran, which was still holding 52 American hostages in flagrant disregard of the United Nations and international law, had no support from any quarter. A number of members of the Council quietly hoped that Iraq's attack, which was originally intended to inflict a crushing defeat on Iran in the first few days, would succeed in bringing down the Khomeini regime.[8] When that failed to materialize, there was a reluctance, especially among the Arab states, to chastise an Arab government while it was fighting the Iranians. Moreover, once the initial shock had subsided, the superpowers and others concluded that their interests could best be served by letting the two regimes exhaust themselves on the battlefield.

As a cold calculation of immediate state interests, that decision may have been warranted. The failure to rise above narrow national interests in the early days of the war, however, tacitly associated the UN Security Council with Iraqi war aims and severely hampered its efforts to forge a peace settlement in later years.

Efforts at negotiation and mediation were left principally to individual states and to the UN secretary general, who appointed Olof Palme as his special representative. Palme focused most of his efforts on attempts to free the many ships trapped in the Shatt al-Arab and to develop a negotiating agenda. The effort to clear the Shatt al-Arab foundered when Iran insisted on joint sponsorship of the operation while Iraq demanded sole responsibility—a rehearsal of the disagreements that reemerged in the 1988 peace talks. Other mediation efforts were initiated by the Islamic Conference Organization and the Non-Aligned Movement. Neither produced any substantial progress.

Continuation of the War: Iran

After the Iraqi attack bogged down in November 1980, a military stalemate ensued until the summer of 1981. From September 1981 through May 1982, Iran conducted three major military offensives that forced Iraq to withdraw to the original border in most places. As Iran's forces approached the border, there was a pause that for the first time seemed to offer opportunities for a negotiated settlement. Consequently, early 1982 was a time of intensive diplomatic contacts and attempted mediation efforts.

Potentially the most important of these efforts was by the government of Algeria, which had not only brokered the original 1975 border agreement but had also demonstrated its diplomatic skills by mediating the release of the US hostages from Iran in January 1981. Algerian Foreign Minister Muhammad Benyahia launched a major effort in early 1982 to seek a diplomatic settlement of the war.

On May 3, while Benyahia's aircraft was in Iranian airspace en route from Turkey to Tehran, his plane was shot down by an air-to-air missile from an Iraqi fighter, killing the foreign minister and all the members of his entourage. An Iraqi pilot captured by Iran years later indicated that the Iraqi objective was to blame Iran for the attack and thereby exacerbate its relations with Algeria.[9] Whatever the motive, the practical effect was that the entire Algerian team of experts who had worked on Iran-Iraq issues since 1975 was killed in a single stroke, and Algeria was effectively removed from the diplomatic scene for more than five years.

Within Iran itself, an intense debate raged about whether to stop at the border or to press its military advantage with an attack into Iraq. In the end, the hardliners won the day. Immediately following the Israeli invasion of Lebanon in early June 1982, Iran announced that its forces were "going to liberate Jerusalem, passing through [the holy city of] Karbala" in Iraq. Shortly thereafter, Iran launched the first of a series of massive offensives intended to break through Iraqi defenses, cut Iraqi supply lines between the south and the capital, and bring down the regime of Saddam Hussein.

Although the Iranians never spelled out the underlying reasons for this decision, it appears to have been a mirror image of the original Iraqi decision to launch its invasion of Khuzistan. Carried away by its own revolutionary hubris, Iran seems to have calculated that the Iraqi military was demoralized and would collapse in the face of a determined attack, that the Shi'i population of southern Iraq would welcome the Iranian army as liberators, that the Iraqi regime would dissolve, and that Iran would emerge as the major power in the Gulf.

The outcome was similarly disastrous. The Iraqi army stiffened in the defense of its homeland, and the conflict quickly degenerated into a war of attrition. In the following years, Iraq began attacking civilian targets in Iran with missiles and aircraft (the "war of the cities"), started missile attacks against Iranian oil shipments (the "tanker war"), and eventually resorted to chemical weapons and poison gas to thwart Iran's massed infantry tactics.

If Iran had chosen to sue for peace in mid-1982, it would have been in a good position to influence the terms of a settlement. At that time, Iran was widely perceived as having snatched victory from the jaws of defeat, and its military forces were regarded as perhaps the most potent in the region. By pursuing peace, Iran could have gone far toward restoring its image with both the regional states and the international community, and it could have established a role for itself as a power broker in the region. Instead, Iran once again chose to let its revolutionary fervor overcome a realistic appraisal of its own long-term interests.

The Diplomatic and Military Dimensions

By mid-1983, Iran's repeated failures to breach Iraqi defenses, combined with the growing effectiveness of the Iraqi air strikes, compelled

Iran to undertake a thorough reappraisal of its diplomatic and military policies. In October 1984, Khomeini summoned Iran's diplomatic representatives from abroad and instructed them to take a new approach:

> We should act as it was done in early Islam when the Prophet . . . sent ambassadors to all parts of the world to establish proper relations. We cannot sit idly by saying we have nothing to do with governments. This is contrary to intellect and religious law. We should have relations with all governments with the exception of a few with which we have no relations at present.[10]

Iranian Prime Minister Mir Hoseyn Musavi expanded on these comments, noting that Iran had experienced difficulties in obtaining spare parts and military equipment because of US pressures. He offered assurances to the nations of the region who had feared the export of Iran's revolution: "We do not want to export armed revolution to any country. That is a big lie. Our aim is to promote the Islamic Revolution through persuasion and by means of truth and courage. These are Islamic values."[11]

This shift in Iran's diplomacy to seek more accommodating relationships with existing governments was accompanied by a shift of comparable magnitude in its military strategy. The speaker of the Majlis, Ali Akbar Hashemi-Rafsanjani, announced at the beginning of 1985 that it was now Iran's intent "to achieve victory with as few casualties as possible."[12] Although Iran had an almost limitless supply of young men, Iran's leaders seemed to have concluded that the bodies of young zealots were no match for Iraqi tanks, aircraft, helicopter gunships, and, on occasion, poison gas.[13] Over the following year, Iran began to rely on small-scale probing actions and guerrilla attacks to harry Iraqi forces.

What was not obvious—to Iraq or to the rest of the world—was Iran's secret preparation of a bold military strike. On February 9, 1986—within days of the seventh anniversary of the revolution—Iran's forces crossed the Shatt al-Arab under cover of a rainstorm, broached Iraqi defenses on the southern flank and occupied the Iraqi port city of Faw.

This brilliant feat of arms was altogether different from earlier Iranian offensives. It was put together with painstaking care and rehearsed over a period of nearly a year. In place of sheer religious fervor, it opted for military professionalism and boldly blended the strengths of Iran's several military organizations. By mid-1986, Khomeini was able to assert that "There was a time when the situation was chaotic and everything was in ruins, but—thank God—everything is now proper and right. . . . Domestic and international affairs are put right."[14]

Khomeini's claim was exaggerated, but when he made that statement he knew—as most of the rest of the world did not—that Iran had succeeded in restoring an arms-supply relationship with the United States. By that time, Iran had received intelligence briefings from the United States on both Iraq and the Soviet Union and had taken delivery of some 1,500 TOW missiles and components for its US-built Hawk air-defense system. Only days before Khomeini's optimistic appraisal, the United States had secretly dispatched Robert C. McFarlane, the former National Security Council adviser, to Tehran to urge Iran's assistance in freeing US hostages in Lebanon and to seek a broader political dialogue with the Islamic revolutionary regime.

Although these shifts in Iran's diplomatic and military strategy paid dividends, they strained the limits of consensus within the revolution. Powerful factions in Iran opposed any apparent softening of revolutionary resolve and continued to view any dealings with the "Great Satan" as treasonous. Perhaps that is what Hashemi-Rafsanjani had in mind when he commented, only one day after Khomeini's declaration that all had been "put right," that "there are at present two relatively powerful factions in our country with differences of view on how the country should be run. . . . They may in fact be regarded as two parties without names."[15]

These two nameless parties were more visible on domestic economic issues than on issues of military and foreign policy. Nevertheless, it was no secret that questions about the appropriate division of labor between the regular military and the Iranian Revolutionary Guards Corps (IRGC or, popularly, the *pasdaran*) sparked fierce debates from the earliest days of the war.

Those differences came to a head in August 1986 when the commander of the Ground Forces, Colonel (later brigadier general) Ali Seyyed Shirazi, had a falling out with his counterpart in the Revolutionary Guards, Mohsen Rezai'e. The two men came to blows, and the issue had to be referred to Khomeini. Shortly thereafter, Shirazi was removed from his post. Shirazi had been one of the key architects of the successful Faw offensive and one of the most important senior military leaders calling for full participation by the professional military in the development of national strategy. His removal in effect left military strategy in the hands of the Revolutionary Guards.

It may be no coincidence that, despite a number of new offensives after August 1986, the Iranian military did not conduct a single successful military operation of any significance from that date until the end of the war.[16] In retrospect, that moment appears to mark the beginning of the deterioration of Iran's military organization and readiness, which led to the routs of early 1988. This would appear to be a third instance in which Iran's revolutionary zeal overcame a sober analysis of its own interests, resulting in severe damage to its domestic and international positions and eventually threatening the integrity of the revolution itself.

The Role of the United States

The policies of the United States throughout the war were equivocal and often contradictory. In the early stages of the war, the United States was among those nations that called for a withdrawal of Iraqi forces, but this position was never pressed at the UN Security Council. Instead, as the war settled into a stalemate, the United States seemed content to accept the international conventional wisdom to keep hands off and let the two sides batter each other.

That attitude began to change after 1982, as Iran went on the offensive and it appeared that Iraq might be defeated and as the tanker war began to inflict costs on the United States and other non-participants. Initially the United States responded to these events by moving closer to Iraq: restoring relations in late 1984, providing Iraq with military intelligence derived from satellites and AWACS reconnaissance, and launching Operation Staunch which was intended to stop the flow of military supplies to Iran. In 1985, however, in an effort to free US hostages in Lebanon and pursue a "strategic opening" to Iran, the United States and Israel began covertly supplying arms to Iran.

When this operation was revealed in late 1986, it not only caused a sensation in the United States but also cast severe doubts on the credibility of all US policies in the Gulf. After a prolonged period of disarray, the United States began to rebuild its tattered relations with the Gulf states in 1987 by intervening more actively on the side of the Arabs and Iraq in the war. Eleven Kuwaiti tankers were permitted to register under the American flag, and US forces in the Gulf were expanded to provide convoy protection against Iranian attacks. In response to mining and missile incidents, US forces directly attacked Iranian ships and oil platforms in October 1987 and April 1988, and US rules of engagement were gradually expanded to permit assistance to virtually any ship attacked by Iran.

Assistant Secretary of State for Near Eastern Affairs Richard Murphy visited Iraq in early 1987 and met with Saddam Hussein on May 11. Murphy reportedly promised Saddam that the United States would lead an effort in the UN Security Council for a resolution calling for a mandatory halt of arms shipments to Iran. According to these reports, the UN resolution would not name Iran directly. Rather, it would first call on Iran and Iraq to agree to a cease-fire and to withdraw their forces to the international boundaries. Then "enforcement measures," such as a worldwide arms embargo, would be imposed on the party that rejected the demand. Iran was expected to reject, Iraq to accept.[17] Over the following months, Murphy's pledge was to become a dominant factor in US policy-making on the war.

Six days after Murphy's visit to Baghdad, the USS *Stark* was struck by Iraqi missiles. That event dramatized the military threat in the Persian Gulf and effectively silenced congressional critics who had been resisting a US naval buildup in the Gulf. The irony of the United States responding to an Iraqi attack by virtually declaring war on Iran was not lost on some observers, but it was soon forgotten in the flood of reports about ship movements, Iranian missile emplacements, and an upsurge of Iranian gunboat and mine attacks on neutral shipping.

Discussions had been under way among the five permanent members of the UN Security Council since January 1987 about a new resolution on the war, and the United States took the lead in these discussions beginning in May.[18] Shortly after Assistant Secretary Murphy's visit to Baghdad, a draft resolution was circulated among the permanent members of the Security Council. As Murphy had promised Saddam Hussein, it was deliberately written in a form that Iran could not accept and included a provision for mandatory sanctions against any party that rejected it.

By June 21, the five permanent members had agreed on a resolution calling for a cease-fire in the war, but they had failed to agree on mandatory sanctions. During the following month, Security Council discussions were expanded to include the non-permanent members, and several changes were introduced, including a provision favored by Iran for establishing an impartial commission to investigate the origins of the war. Resolution 598 was adopted unanimously by the UN Security Council on July 20, 1987.

Iran, unexpectedly, did not reject the resolution. Instead, Iran offered to observe a cease-fire if, first, in accordance with paragraph six of the resolution, a commission were formed to determine who started the war.[19] Iraq rejected this offer as "invalid," insisting that the resolution had to be implemented in the order of the paragraphs and that paragraph six could not be invoked until the preceding five paragraphs, including full Iranian withdrawal, had been carried out. Shortly thereafter, Iraq resumed full-scale attacks on Iranian cities and ships. Thus, between September 1987 and February 1988, the fighting continued essentially because of a difference between the parties over the order of implementation of the paragraphs of Resolution 598. The United States chose to ignore the signals coming from Iran, and, in accordance with its previous understanding, devoted its efforts to achieving an arms embargo against Iran.

As president of the Security Council during February, the United States announced its intention to move toward a "showdown," but was unable to muster the necessary support.[20] On February 29, as the United States relinquished the Security Council presidency, Iraq dramatically escalated the war. On that evening, Iraq fired 11 modified

SCUD B missiles at Tehran. A total of more than 100 such missiles were fired in the following two weeks at Tehran, Qom, and Isfahan, together with extensive bombing raids against 37 Iranian cities, decisively ending any opportunity to test the Iranian offer of a negotiated cease-fire.[21]

Could the war have been ended by a compromise in early 1988? The answer will never be known, primarily because the United States was unwilling to explore Iran's offer. The US position—and sensitivities about even the perception of any sympathy toward Iran—were a direct legacy of the Iran-contra fiasco. They may have contributed to prolonging the war for six unnecessary months.

Final Straws

Throughout the spring and summer of 1988, evidence accumulated of growing factional disputes within the Iranian leadership. Elections for the third Majlis in early April were extremely contentious. In the days immediately preceding the election, a Kuwaiti airliner was hijacked to Mashhad, severely embarrassing those elements of the leadership who were attempting to cleanse Iran's image as a "terrorist state." Several days later, mines again appeared in the central Persian Gulf, one of which struck the USS *Samuel B. Roberts* and set off a new round of clashes with US forces. Hashemi-Rafsanjani characterized this incident as "An accident . . . which appears to be rigged by elements we cannot yet identify."[22]

This was only the beginning of a series of blows that Iran experienced over a period of three months. Iraq went on the offensive against Iran's disorganized and disheartened military forces, recaptured the Faw peninsula in a lightning attack on April 18, then proceeded to push back Iranian forces all along the front. In mid-May, Iraq carried out a devastating attack on the Iranian oil-transfer site at Larak Island in the southern gulf, destroying five ships, including the world's largest supertanker. Anti-war sentiment began to appear openly in demonstrations in major Iranian cities and, most disturbing of all for the divided leadership, persuasive evidence began to accumulate that Khomeini was severely ill and virtually incapacitated.

Iran desperately attempted to stem the tide, appointing Hashemi-Rafsanjani as the acting commander in chief in an effort to halt the disarray and disintegration of the armed forces and starting a new peace offensive at the United Nations. This was interrupted, however, on July 3 by the tragic downing of a commercial Iranian aircraft by the USS *Vincennes*, killing all 290 passengers and crew.

This terrible accident, coming at the end of a seemingly endless series of defeats, underscored the despair of Iran's position. Despite the enormity of the mistake, Iran was unable to muster sufficient support at the UN to condemn the US action. Its isolation and weakness were never more apparent. As Hashemi-Rafsanjani noted just before the Airbus incident, "We created enemies for ourselves [in the international community]. . . . We have not spent enough time seeing that they become friends."[23]

On July 18, Iranian Foreign Minister Ali Akbar Vilayati sent a letter to UN Secretary General Perez de Cuellar formally accepting Resolution 598. Although Iran did not spell out the reasons for this decision, the key factor was probably the changed conditions at the battlefront. Iran had always balked at withdrawing its forces from Iraqi territory without some quid pro quo. That consideration had now been rendered moot by Iraq's recapture of virtually all of its own territory. Resolution 598 had originally been written to favor Iraq, which in mid-1987 was perceived as in danger of losing the war. With the change of fortune on the battlefield, the resolution now offered the prospect of international support and protection for Iran in the face of an effective and determined Iraqi offensive.

Iraq was taken by surprise and initially resisted accepting a cease-fire while continuing its mopping-up operations. Iraq also continued to demonstrate a contemptuous disregard for the Security Council and for world opinion on the use of chemical weapons. A UN investigative team reported to the Security Council on August 1 that "chemical weapons continue to be used on an intensive scale" by Iraq. Only hours later, Iraq launched a massive chemical bombing attack on the

Iranian town of Oshnoviyeh. As international pressure mounted, however, Saddam Hussein finally agreed on August 6 to accept a cease-fire on the condition that it would be followed immediately by direct talks. A UN observer force was rushed to the region, and a cease-fire went into effect on August 20. Formal talks began in Geneva on August 25, under the aegis of the UN secretary general. Although the war was not over, for the first time in eight years fighting was suspended.

In this sorry litany of blunders, the final place of honor must go to Iraq. By its decision to back away from the United States once its victory seemed assured,[24] by its recalcitrance in accepting Resolution 598, by its imposition of preconditions on peace negotiations, by its unwillingness to accept the negotiating agenda developed by Perez de Cuellar, and most of all by its use of chemical weapons after Iran had accepted the cease-fire—first against Iranian civilian targets and then against its own Kurdish population[25]—Iraq managed to dissipate within a period of only a few weeks much of the support that it had managed to attract throughout the last years of the war.

Largely by its own actions, Iraq contributed to a remarkable reversal of roles, in which Iran began to appear as the more reasonable and cooperative of the two parties. Clearly, Iraq emerged from the war as the military superpower of the Gulf, but its behavior almost immediately began to arouse apprehensions among its neighbors, who quickly took steps to repair some of their ties with Tehran. It remains to be seen how Iraq will use the regional power and influence that it acquired during the eight years of the war.

Observations

After this selective look back, it is worth considering the implications of this situation over the next few years, particularly from the perspective of US policy. One of the major difficulties of US policy in the recent past has been the unstated assumption that it was necessary to choose between Iran and Iraq. Perhaps that has been true at times, but it need not be true in the future if the fighting is contained.

Both Iraq and Iran are crucial to any long-term US strategy in the

Gulf. Iraq's oil reserves are second only to those of Saudi Arabia, which probably ensures that it will play a major role in regional politics and international energy issues for at least the next half-century. In addition, Iraq has a solid agricultural base and a skilled and resourceful population, giving it the potential to be a strong and independent presence once freed of the immense drain of the war.

Iran's oil reserves, though substantial, will dwindle more quickly than those of either Iraq or Saudi Arabia. Iran's natural gas reserves are immense, however, perhaps second only to those of the Soviet Union. Iran, the largest country in the region in geography and population, dominates the entire northern coast of the Persian Gulf and lies between the Gulf and the Soviet Union. It, too, has the potential to play a major role in both regional and international affairs over the next half-century and beyond.

The problem for the United States—and for the industrialized nations generally—has been the political leadership of these two states. Iran's leadership, particularly since the revolution, has been quixotic and immensely disruptive on virtually every regional and international issue. It is in the throes of an internal power struggle that may yet explode—now that Khomeini has passed from the scene—with essentially unpredictable consequences.

Iraq is governed by a small circle of Baathist leaders under the absolute personal control of Saddam Hussein. Politically, it is one of the most closed societies in the Middle East. Its policy-making is highly idiosyncratic and is characterized by a clandestine, almost furtive quality. In the past, Iraq has also played a subversive and destabilizing role in regional affairs.

The United States can take little pride in its policies toward either of these difficult regimes. Washington has been clumsy and inconsistent, and its policies have tended to vacillate between extremes. Over the next several years, as these two states turn toward issues of domestic reconstruction and reintegration into a more constructive system of relationships with their neighbors, the United States and other external powers may have a unique opportunity to redefine their long-term interests and devise more sensible and constructive policies to pursue them. This is not the place to propose such a strategy. Based on this brief review of the dismal record by all parties over the past several years, however, it does seem appropriate to hope that they will benefit from their past mistakes and reduce both their interventionist tendencies and their expectations.

NOTES

1. Iranian spokesmen often refer to the river as the Arvand, in part to avoid any suggestion of Arab sovereignty, just as the Arabs often refer to the Persian Gulf as the Arabian Gulf.

2. Iran did not formally announce its adherence to the 1975 treaty until October 26, 1980, more than a month after the war had begun.

3. For a detailed treatment of this period, see R.K. Ramazani, *Revolutionary Iran* (Baltimore: The Johns Hopkins University Press, 1986), especially chapter 4. For a primarily legal interpretation drawn largely from Iraqi sources, see Majid Khadduri, *The Gulf War: The Origins and Implications of the Iran-Iraq Conflict* (New York: Oxford University Press, 1988).

4. J.B. Moore, *International Adjudications, Ancient and Modern* (Washington, DC: Government Printing Office, 1929-1933), p. 5043.

5. Foreign Broadcast Information Service, *Daily Report—South Asia* (FBIS-SA), Washington, DC, September 26, 1980, cited in R.K. Ramazani, *Revolutionary Iran*, p. 61.

6. Foreign Office (Iraq), *Documentary Dossier* (Baghdad, 1981), p. 212, cited in Khadduri, *Gulf War*, p. 85.

7. For a concise summary of UN activities during the war, see the paper by Ralph King in "The United Nations and the Iran-Iraq War," ed. Brian Urquhart and Gary Sick (New York: Ford Foundation Conference Report, August 1987), pp. 7-27.

8. Iraqi Ambassador to the UN Ismat Kittani was able to delay the first formal Security Council meeting on the war by promising that Iraq would quickly "solve" the problem (*ibid.*, p. 29). Arab sources who were in contact with the Iraqi leadership in the first days of the war claimed privately that Iraq's war strategy was consciously modeled on Israel's six-day campaign in 1967.

9. An Iraqi Mirage pilot, Captain Zuhayr Muhammad Said al-Audisi, was captured by Iran on February 2, 1987, when his plane crashed in Iranian territory. He reportedly told Iranian interrogators that an Iraqi MiG-25 fighter piloted by Lt. Col. Abdullah Faraj was ordered in early May 1982 to fly toward the Iranian-Turkish border where the Iraqi government knew that Algerian Foreign Minister Benyahia's aircraft would pass. The aircraft was shot down with a Soviet air-to-air missile. (FBIS-SA, May 22, 1987, p. I-3).

10. FBIS-SA, October 30, 1984, p. I-1.

11. *Ibid.*, p. I-2.

12. *Ibid.*, February 6, 1985, p. I-2.

13. By the end of the war, Iran had approximately 1 million men in the active military and reserves, representing about 17 percent of Iranian men between the ages of 18 and 32. Iraq had about 1.6 million men on active duty and reserves, representing virtually 100 percent of Iraqi men 18-32. See *The Military Balance 1988-1989* (London: International Institute of Strategic Studies, 1988), pp. 100-101.

14. FBIS-SA, June 9, 1986, p. I-2.

15. Public address on June 10, 1986. FBIS-SA, June 11, 1986, p. I-3.

16. The most significant offensive during that period was the campaign to capture Basra in January 1987. The vigorous and successful Iraqi defense of Basra against Iran's best military efforts was probably instrumental in persuading the Iranian leaders that their original hopes of winning the war were no longer realistic, thereby contributing to a further decline in morale.

17. *Washington Post*, May 30 and 31, 1987. These reports were based on a background briefing at the State Department, apparently with Murphy.

18. Consideration of a major new UN initiative on the war had begun through the efforts of Secretary General Javier Perez de Cuellar in 1985. The British delegation took the lead in promoting such an initiative in early 1986, until the United States became directly engaged in May, about the time of the Murphy trip to Baghdad.

19. The most authoritative statement of the positions of the two parties was presented in the secretary general's report to the Security Council on September 16, 1987. Although the report was confidential, it circulated widely at the United Nations and was published verbatim by the Kuwait News Agency on September 19. FBIS-Near East and South Asia (NES), September 22, 1987, p. 45.

20. President Ronald Reagan told Saudi Foreign Minister Saud in Washington that the United States was "committed to a major effort this month while we serve as president of the Security Council." *Washington Post*, February 10, 1988, p. 32. Secretary of State George Shultz reportedly raised this with the Soviets during his visit to Moscow in late February, presenting a plan that would involve a quick vote on the second resolution but with a 30-day delay in implementation to permit more time for the secretary general to pursue negotiations. *Washington Post*, February 25, 1988, p. 36.

21. On February 28, 1988 the Iranian foreign minister sent a formal letter to the UN secretary general confirming Iran's acceptance of the secretary general's implementation plan for a cease-fire, which he said was "tantamount to the acceptance of Resolution 598." This statement had been negotiated by several members of the Security Council over a period of weeks and was regarded in Iran as a major concession. Because of the Iraqi missile attack on the following day, it received no attention outside UN circles.

22. Interview on April 18. FBIS-NES, April 19, 1988, p. 59.

23. Interview on July 2. FBIS-NES, July 6, 1988, p. 60.

24. As early as May 1988, Saddam Hussein refused to meet with Vernon Walters, the US ambassador to the United Nations, during a visit to Baghdad and launched a full-scale propaganda campaign against US policies, apparently in response to US opposition to Iraq's use of chemical weapons. On the eve of the Walters' visit, Iraqi First Deputy Prime Minister Taha Yasin Ramadan told *al-Musawwar* (Cairo). "We say that in defending our territories, we will use all types of weapons. Those who oppose this can do whatever they like . . . we reject any move by the international community to ask us not to use certain weapons." FBIS-NES, May 24, 1988, p. 18.

25. Iraq stoutly denied that chemical weapons were used in the campaign against the Kurds. The United States claimed to have intelligence indicating that such weapons were used. Responsible Turkish authorities, in private discussions with the author in the fall of 1988, confirmed the likelihood of chemical attacks, if only on a scale intended to panic the Kurdish population into fleeing from their villages and military positions.

Challenges for
US Policy

R. K. Ramazani

During its first decade, the Iranian Revolution posed formidable challenges to US foreign policy. The principal challenges were the taking of American hostages, the secret arms deal, and the conduct of a quasi-war with the United States in the Persian Gulf.

The Hostage Dispute

Challenge begets challenge. That is exactly why for 444 days the holding of American hostages by Iranian students preoccupied the Washington policy community, agonized the families of the American hostages, antagonized the American public, and ultimately contributed to President Jimmy Carter's electoral defeat. The president himself was the first American to throw down the gauntlet by allowing the overthrown shah to enter the United States on October 22, 1979. Conspiracy theories notwithstanding, the president's decision was influenced primarily by humanitarian concerns. Here are the essential facts: At first the president extended an invitation for the shah to come to the United States on the assumption that it would be acted upon immediately in January 1979, when he left Tehran. When State Department officials judged that Americans might be held hostage for the return of the shah, the president reluctantly withdrew the invitation. Not until October did the president learn that the shah was gravely ill. Until then the shah had traveled to several countries, from Egypt

125

westward to Mexico. Meanwhile Washington and Tehran negotiated for nearly 10 months to establish relations on a new basis, and the president felt no need to reiterate his invitation. The president's humanitarian concern was as evident after the shah came to the United States as it had been before. In a meeting at the White House on December 10, 1979, this author witnessed how the president bristled at the idea that the shah might have to be extradited as a means of resolving the hostage dispute.

Yet, Carter's decision clearly misgauged the intensity of the Iranian reaction. Warren Christopher, deputy secretary of state and chief negotiator of the hostage settlement, lamented the failure of the American media to understand the "hatred of the Iranians for the United States . . . against the background of gross and prolonged abuses by the Shah and the history of U.S. involvement with him. . . ."[1] Christopher's perceptive remarks refer particularly to the Iranian people's bitter memory of how the Central Intelligence Agency (CIA) destroyed the popular government of Muhammad Mossadegh in August 1953, an action which led to the shah's return to power after he had fled the country. Against the backdrop of such CIA machinations, Ayatollah Ruhollah Khomeini believed that even the news of the shah's grave illness "might actually be a plot." He was not alone in this belief. Moderates and militants, realists and idealists, nationalists and Islamicists, and leftists and rightists alike feared that the United States would repeat the 1953 coup plot.

The American hostages were held partly as a guarantee that Washington would not repeat such mischief, but the Iranians failed to understand that they, too, could be held hostage. Thanks to the shah's overdependence on the United States, billions of Iranian dollars had been deposited in American banks. With Executive Order 12170, Carter froze Iranian funds on November 14, 1979. Ironically, Abol Hasan Bani-Sadr's ill-considered talk of withdrawing Iran's funds provided the final impetus for the US freeze. Contrary to the general perception, the president ordered the freeze only partly as a means of pressuring Iran to free the American hostages. He was also motivated by political and economic considerations. Politically, he believed that the United

States could not remain passive indefinitely in the face of hostile Iranian acts; and economically, he sensed the need to protect the many US claimants.

The hostility toward Iran that the hostage crisis generated in the United States almost completely overshadowed the constructive moves that Iran made both during and after the settlement of the dispute. During the crisis, it was Iran that took the initiative of secretly opening the "bankers' channel" to negotiate with the Americans. Ironically, this channel developed out of Iranian litigations against the United States. Iran's German lawyers met with American lawyers on May 15, 1980 in a small town near Frankfurt and began negotiations that would lead to a pragmatic economic solution to the international litigation. The secret Iranian initiative seems all the more remarkable considering that on April 7, 1980 President Carter had broken diplomatic relations with Iran and had imposed unilateral economic sanctions; more critically, the United States had launched a military operation into Iran on April 24, 1980 in an attempt to rescue the American hostages. It was also as the result of the Iranian initiative that on September 9, 1980 the indirect channel of negotiations between Iran and the United States was opened; Sadeq Tabatabai, an in-law of Khomeini's, contacted German Ambassador Gerhard Ritzel in Tehran, informing him that Iran was prepared to release the hostages on certain conditions. Those conditions, set forth in Khomeini's speech of September 12, became the general basis for negotiations between the two sides. With the help of skillful Algerian intermediaries a settlement of the dispute was reached.

Iran's desire to protect its international financial credibility and eventually to reestablish relations with the United States is also evidenced by its businesslike behavior in settling the claims US nationals brought against it before the Iran-US Claims Tribunal at The Hague, starting on October 20, 1981. By October 24, 1988, the Tribunal had issued 396 awards, amounting to about $906 million for US claimants and only about $70 million for Iranian parties. More than 400 US companies and individuals have sued Iran since the revolution.[2] According to various US newspaper reports, Iran has paid many bank claimants—the Export-Import Bank, for example, which received $419.5 million in 1983. It has also paid many nonbank claimants, including more than 130 US companies.

By any revolutionary state's standards, the Iranian settlement of foreign claims has been exemplary. Parties that filed claims after World War II or the Chinese Revolution have waited decades to win judgments and have often had difficulty collecting their awards. A Delaware company, for example, had to wait 29 years to settle its claim against the People's Republic of China for a power plant expropriated after the Chinese Revolution. By contrast, according to the US Treasury Department and banking officials associated with negotiations with Iran, the talks "with Iranian representatives have been business-like, realistic and pragmatic."[3] Such negotiations were carried out despite the fact that Iranian leaders such as Majlis Speaker Ali Akbar Hashemi-Rafsanjani continue to assert that Iran's assets in the United States have been frozen illegally and urge the United States to show its good will by releasing those assets.

The Arms Deal

The American hostages in Iran were finally released in January 1981, but others were held—and some continue to be held—by pro-Iranian Shi'i factions in Lebanon. Hopes of gaining their release lay at the heart of the Reagan administration's scandalous arms deal with Iran. In the three years since the beginning of the Iran-contra affair, countless documents have been examined and reexamined by the three branches of the US government in efforts to ascertain how and why officials in the National Security Council and the CIA usurped control of US policy toward Iran—and to determine who should be punished for violating the law.

Yet a careful scrutiny of the record reveals that the arms deal stemmed from an Iranian initiative; hence, once again, as in the hostage dispute, it was revolutionary Iran that posed a challenge to US foreign policy. Iran's America initiative emerged from the converging effects of Iran's domestic revolutionary politics and its protracted war with Iraq. Having consolidated their power by 1985, the Khomeinist factions, particularly the realist or pragmatic elements among them, had launched an "open-door" foreign policy. This policy sought to strike a balance between the requirements of Iran's national interest and its Islamic ideology. It favored establishing ties with other governments despite the opposition of the revolutionary idealists who insisted on maintaining relative isolation in world politics, presumably as a means of protecting Iran's ideological purity. While it lasted, this flexible foreign policy orientation allowed such moves as the arms deal with the United States, although these remained secret, indirect, and fully deniable.

The effects of the war with Iraq similarly prompted Iranian overtures toward the United States. Faced with the continued US arms embargo, with dependency on US military equipment and spare parts, and with Iraq's ever-growing arsenal, Iran's need for American arms and spare parts was overwhelming. Hence, the phrase "arms-for-hostages" accurately describes the *overriding and immediate* objectives of Iran *and* the United States. Iran received six shipments of arms, beginning on August 30, 1985 and ending on November 6, 1986, only three days after the Lebanese magazine *al-Shiraa* disclosed the secret mission of former NSC adviser Robert C. McFarlane to Iran. In the meantime, three American hostages—the Reverend Benjamin Weir, the Reverend Laurence Martin Jenco, and David P. Jacobson—were released by their Lebanese captors.

But the phrase "arms-for-hostages" fails to describe the *long-term* objectives of either the United States or Iran. Just as Washington had shown restraint when American hostages were taken—in part to retain the option of reestablishing relations with strategically important Iran—in the course of arms sales discussions it hoped to contruct a "strategic opening" to Iran. Iran's long-term objectives were no less real, although they are less well known. In the course of the hostage dispute, and more so after its settlement, Iran sought to leave the door ajar for renewing relations with Washington at a later date. Iran also sought to broaden the arms-deal discussions with the United

States to include US cooperation in the defense of Iran against possible Soviet invasion and in assistance to the Afghan resistance movement.

Traumatized by the memory of what befell former prime minister Mehdi Bazargan after his November 1979 meeting with Zbigniew Brzezinski, the Iranian leaders to a man vehemently denied that Iran had ever purchased US arms or that its "officials" had ever talked to US officials. Technically, they were correct. Their covert transactions were conducted through such intermediaries as the wheeler-dealer Manuchehr Ghorbanifar. Fearing the reactions of hot-headed idealists who had raised anti-Americanism to the level of a religio-political doctrine, the Iranian leaders made sure that no American-style legislative investigation would ever be attempted. When, in November 1986, eight deputies of the Majlis demanded a parliamentary investigation into what had transpired between Iran and the United States, Imam Khomeini quashed the request. He admonished the deputies, saying that they "should not set up radicals and reactionaries. . . . This is contrary to Islam. . . . Do not do such things." That was the end of the matter.

Yet, despite all the denials and invective, no Iranian leader ever slammed the door shut on the United States. The best example is the statement of Speaker Hashemi-Rafsanjani in the wake of the startling disclosure of the arms deal. Despite all his mocking, belittling, and denouncing of Washington, he managed to imply sympathy for the beleaguered American president and repeatedly offered to use Iran's influence to free American hostages. On November 4, 1986, commemorating the capture of the US embassy in Tehran, he addressed the United States in these words, "If you wish us to intercede on your behalf, we have left the door open."[4] He also left the door open to normalizing relations with the United States. In his reply to a CBS correspondent on January 28, 1987, Hashemi-Rafsanjani said, "There is only one condition [for normalizing relations]: The United States must prove that it is not hostile to our people, government, and revolution" by, for instance, releasing Iranian assets as proof of American good will.

Armed Conflict

In Iranian eyes, the lack of US good will toward Iran was clearly demonstrated in repeated armed attacks on Iranian targets in the Persian Gulf. At no time since the Vietnam War had the United States deployed such massive naval forces as when, on July 22, 1987, it started escorting American-flagged Kuwaiti oil tankers in Gulf waters. President Ronald Reagan's controversial decision to reflag Kuwaiti tankers was attributed variously to embarrassment over the secret arms deals with Iran (undertaken in direct contravention of its advocacy of an arms embargo against Tehran), to its commitment to the principle of freedom of navigation, and (according to President Reagan's hyperbole of May 19, 1987) to the defense of Western freedom and security and assurance of the uninterrupted flow of Gulf oil supplies to world markets. Although embarrassment over the arms deal did influence the reflagging decision, the record reveals that the primary objective was to preempt a large-scale Soviet operation of escorting Kuwaiti vessels. Former Secretary of Defense Caspar Weinberger believed that an American refusal to honor the Kuwaiti request, in the face of the Kuwaiti appeal for help from Moscow, "would have created a vacuum in the Gulf into which Soviet power would shortly have been projected."[5] The Kuwaitis played cleverly on the Reagan administration's fear of the "Evil Empire" to get the Americans to outdo the Soviets in escorting their vessels. As *Washington Post* columnist Stephen S. Rosenfeld characterized it, "Little Kuwait Wins the Brilliant and Gutsy Diplomacy Award."

Regardless of American motivations, the net effect of the US naval escorting operations was to limit Iran's retaliatory power against Iraq's attacks on Iranian oil shipments. In the absence of Iraqi vessels traversing Gulf waters, Iran attacked the oil shipments of Kuwait and Saudi Arabia, Iraq's principal financial and logistical allies. US efforts to protect non-Iranian oil shipments during the war between Iran and Iraq inevitably led to a quasi-war between Tehran and Washington. This conflict ran from July 24, 1987—when the *Bridgeton*, a Kuwaiti supertanker flying the US flag, struck a mine—to July 3, 1988, when the USS *Vincennes* accidentally shot down an Iranian Airbus A-300 passenger plane en route from Bandar Abbas to Dubai, killing 290 passengers and crew. In the meantime, US retaliatory attacks on Iranian targets—particularly the April 1988 strike that destroyed the Sassan and Nasr oil platforms on Iran's Sirri Island and crippled much of the Iranian Navy—left deep psychological wounds. From the start, Iran had seen America's hand in Iraq's invasion of Iran. Now US military intervention in the Persian Gulf seemed to confirm all Iranian suspicions about US-Iraqi collusion against Iran.

The US-Iranian armed conflict was also accompanied by diplomatic and economic warfare. After the adoption of Resolution 598 by the United Nations Security Council in July 1987, Washington strove to put diplomatic pressure on Iran to accept the resolution, threatening to impose a UN-sponsored arms embargo. Iran managed to fend off the threat by playing the Soviet and Chinese cards and by dangling the prospects of improved relations before the eyes of Britain and France. Washington also supported the adoption of anti-Iranian resolutions in the UN Security Council in 1984, 1986, and 1987, partly instigated by US friends in the Gulf Cooperation Council (GCC). The GCC states also engineered an unprecedented condemnation of Iran at the Arab summit meeting at Amman in November 1987. To Washington's pleasant surprise, even Syria, Iran's major Arab ally, joined in the Arab world's denunciation of Iran.

Pressured by the Congress, the Reagan administration imposed a trade ban on Iran on October 30, 1987. The decision was prompted in part by Iran's missile attack on Kuwait's Sea Island oil terminal four days earlier. The House and Senate voted overwhelmingly to ban imports, particularly oil, from Iran when they discovered that in 1986 Iran had exported about $500 million worth of crude oil to the United States. The administration imposed an embargo on US imports from Iran and a ban on 14 kinds of "militarily useful" items previously exported to Iran. Some US officials believed that the ban might contravene the Algiers Accords which had settled the hostage dispute, but legal niceties could neither diminish nor deter the ongoing military, diplomatic, and economic conflict between Tehran and Washington.

Yet, in spite of the conflict, Iranian leaders managed to retain the option of normalizing relations with Washington. President Ali Khamenei's much-heralded speech of September 22, 1987 to the UN General Assembly was meant to be a step in that direction, but its expected benign political effects were ruined on September 21 when a US Navy helicopter fired on the *Iran Ajr*, which the Reagan administration charged was laying underwater mines. Less than a month later, however, when a correspondent of the *Tehran Times* asked Khamenei, "If the United States were to halt its enmity and return Iranian assets, would these constitute conditions in which ties could be established?" he replied, "Certainly there are conditions where our ties with the United States could be normalized. Of course, they include those conditions you have already mentioned, and perhaps there would be others."

The prospects for normalizing US-Iranian relations seemed to improve after Khomeini's acceptance of UN Resolution 598 on July 18, 1988. Domestically, Khomeini's decision appeared to favor the position of revolutionary realist factions. Iran's relations with Britain, France, Canada, and other Western nations began to improve rapidly, and the revolutionary realists helped secure the release of seven French and German hostages in Lebanon. Major Iranian leaders emphasized the importance of reconstruction at home rather than export of revolution abroad. The signs of Iran's improving relations with Western Europe encouraged President George Bush to offer Iran an olive branch in his inaugural address, indicating that Tehran's assistance in releasing the hostages in Lebanon "will be long remembered. Good will begets good will. Good faith can be a spiral that endlessly moves on." The air of optimism about the prospects of improving relations with Iran was so pervasive in Washington that even the cautious Congressman Lee H. Hamilton, in addressing a Middle East Institute conference in Washington on February 4, 1989, insisted, "We must start talking with Iran," even if the United States had to pick up the phone and call Iran first.

The Rushdie Affair

On February 14, 1989, Khomeini's imposition of a death sentence on Salman Rushdie, author of *The Satanic Verses*, burst the bubble of excessive optimism about Iran's return to the Western fold. Iran severed diplomatic relations with Britain on March 7, 1989, apparently scrapping the laboriously worked-out November 9, 1988 memorandum of understanding between Tehran and London, which had formed the basis of their newly resumed diplomatic relations. Iran recalled its representatives from European Community nations in reaction to the recall of their envoys from Tehran; shortly thereafter Deputy Foreign Minister for Euro-American Affairs Muhammad Javad Larijani and UN envoy Muhammad Jaafar Mahallati resigned, supposedly because they had favored early improvement of US-Iranian relations. Western astonishment over Iran's sudden about-face peaked on May 5, 1989, when the revolutionary realist *par excellence*, Speaker Hashemi-Rafsanjani, declared in a Friday sermon on Jerusalem Day, "If for every one Palestinian today, they execute five Americans, or English, or French—outside Palestine, not inside—such wrongdoings will not be repeated. It is not difficult to kill the French or Americans, although it is somewhat difficult to kill the Israelis, as they are a bit scarce."[6]

From a linear perspective of Iranian foreign policy, all this seemed incredible against the backdrop of considerable improvement in Iranian-Western relations over a period of nearly nine months between Khomeini's acceptance of the cease-fire and his death edict against Rushdie. From the kaleidoscopic perspective described in "Iran's Foreign Policy" (in this volume), however, such a sudden shift might have been expected. Before explaining why, it must be stated unambiguously that not only as a devout Muslim, but also as the perceived "source of emulation" (*marja'a-e taqlid*) of the world's Shi'i community and the perceived "Imam of the Muslim community" (*imam-e ummat*), Khomeini's outrage over the publication of *The Satanic Verses* as a blasphemous novel might have been expected.

Khomeini's action may be seen also in terms of his role as the supreme arbiter of Iranian affairs. As seen in "Iran's Foreign Policy," in accepting the UN cease-fire resolution (Resolution 598), he in effect threw his weight behind the realist factions; under the circumstances this appeared to insure the survival of his Islamic Revolution. The apparent stampeding of the realist factions to improve ties with the West seems to have alarmed the ideological factions. Rushdie's death sentence was, in effect, an attempt to redress the balance. This interpretation is supported by Khomeini's "very important" (in the official Iranian appellation) address of February 22, 1989, in which for the first time he spoke about his role as the balancer among factions; for the first time, he admonished those who act "in a pragmatic way"; and he cautioned against becoming dependent on the West, saying, "It is not necessary for us to pursue the establishment of extensive ties [with the West]. . . ."[7]

In practice, as well as by definition, Khomeini's balancing act signified neither his abandonment of the realist factions nor opposition to their pursuit of ties with the West. To be sure, Iranian leaders have intensified efforts to forge ties with the Soviet Union and other communist nations since the deterioration of relations with Western nations. Several events—including Soviet Foreign Minister Eduard Shevardnadze's Tehran visit of February 25–27, 1989, arranged before the Rushdie row; the June 1989 visit of Hashemi-Rafsanjani to the Soviet Union; President Khamenei's visit to China; and new arms deals with Czechoslovakia, Romania, and other communist nations— appear to mean a definite tilt toward the East at the expense of the West.

Yet Iran's "neither East nor West" guideline defies such a zero-sum game. Iran has already received the envoys of European Community nations who returned on their own initiative. Iran continues to recognize its dependence on foreign expertise, especially in such sectors as the petrochemical industry, in which various companies from Italy, Germany, Holland, France, and England have already declared willingness to participate. Also, as before the Rushdie furor, Iran continues to retain the option of forging ties with the United States under certain conditions. The official Tehran Domestic Service stated on April 9, 1989 that from "the Islamic Republic's view, the resumption of ties [with the US] is not possible or practical—unless, for instance, hostile confrontations are abandoned, the values and principles of the Islamic revolution are respected, and our frozen assets are freed."[8]

The Future

What seems certain about the challenges of revolutionary Iran to US policy is that in the future, as in the past, these challenges will stem from an acute interplay of external environment and conditions within Iran. Although the basic elements of both categories may be identified, at the moment they are by no means predictable. Regarding the external environment, the "cool war" (rather than the Cold War) between Washington and Moscow may promote the establishment both of peace between Iran and Iraq and of regional security in the Persian Gulf, but no one knows how durable current improvements in superpower relations will be. The Bush administration seems to be less antagonistic toward revolutionary Iran than was the Reagan administration, but no one knows if this will mean greater creativity in building a constructive relationship with Tehran. The threat of a proliferation of ballistic missiles and of biological, chemical, and nuclear weapons is being addressed—in the case of ballistic missiles, by the seven Western nations that signed the US-sponsored Missile Technology Control Regime in 1987. No one knows, however, whether any global efforts for nonproliferation of these weapons will stem the growing race for arms under way in the Persian Gulf.

The consequences of an unfinished revolution and an unwon war have created horrendous economic and political problems for Iranian leaders, making Iran's domestic affairs as unpredictable as its external environment. As the world's second largest natural gas producer, as well as an oil- and mineral-rich nation, Iran holds considerable economic potential. No less important, as President Khamenei pointed out upon his return from a visit to China in May 1989, the Iranian Revolution has survived without outside support as contrasted with the Chinese Revolution, which received early Soviet aid. In addition, unlike Iraq, Iran has weathered the mammoth financial costs of nearly eight years of war without incurring any foreign debt.

Yet the fact remains that the single most important socioeconomic promise of the revolution—that is, improving the miserable lot of the poorer masses—remains unfulfilled. The staggering price increases, the persistent 35-40 percent annual inflation rate, and the unresolved dispute over priorities among private, public, and cooperative sectors continue to haunt Iran amid growing demands for better wages and salaries. Before the cease-fire, many of these and other social and economic problems were blamed on the "imposed war," but such a rationale no longer exists. More critically, the need for socioeconomic reforms have been compounded by the necessity of massive postwar reconstruction. Even Iran's much-heralded ability to avoid foreign indebtedness must be weighed against its heavy borrowing from the country's own banking system, a practice that has had a negative effect on inflation.

What seems encouraging is that in finally launching its first five-year development plan 10 years after the revolution, Iranian planners have at least admitted that their earlier planning attempts, as in 1982, never got off the ground because of "far-fetched" estimates of anticipated oil income and an "absence of realistic goals." This first plan aims at an increase of about 5.5 percent in the GNP from 1989 to 1993. Taking account of the average 3.2 percent population growth, a 2.3 percent growth for the per capita GNP is envisioned.[9] At least two problems, however, need to be mentioned: The plan is based on the assumption that the country's oil income will be $63 billion during the five-year period, but the 1986 slump in oil prices is a bitter reminder of the unpredictability of such prices. Equally important is the persistent problem of a dearth of skilled workers in an emerging anti-entrepreneurial climate, this despite the call of some Iranian leaders for the return of the nation's talented and skilled self-exiled citizens.

The political problems that face Iran are equally unpredictable. In the past, Iranians have rationalized them, again, partly in terms of the "imposed war." More realistically, they now acknowledge that the lack of political experience on the part of the drafters of the constitution led to the excessive dispersion of power in the executive and the judiciary. The key political problem facing Iran at the turn of the second decade of its revolution, however, is the problem of succession, which first arose on March 27, 1989, when the presumed successor to Khomeini, Ayatollah Hoseyn Ali Montazeri, resigned from his position of deputy leader on the ground of "unpreparedness" (*adam-e amadegi*). In a March 28 letter accepting Montazeri's resignation, Khomeini revealed that relations between the mentor and his former student had become strained, at least since the arrest in 1986 of Mehdi Hashemi, brother of Montazeri's son-in-law. Without being specific, Khomeini accused Montazeri of keeping company with such "liberals" as former prime minister Bazargan and of listening to antirevolutionary "hypocrites"—the Mujahidin-e Khalq, the main opponents of the Khomeini government. He warned Montazeri, "cleanse your household of unsuitable individuals, and seriously prevent the comings and goings of opponents of the system who pretend to support Islam and the Islamic Republic."[10]

Theories explaining Montazeri's forced resignation abound. Suffice it to say that the official line denies what was probably the principal reason for his dismissal—Montazeri's strident criticism of government policies. He boldly accused the government of suppressing civil and political liberties, conducting large-scale purges, and meting out imprisonment and executions without due process of law. The government accused him of "incredulity," "gullibility," and "simplemindedness," discrediting his criticisms on the ground that he was, in effect, parroting the accusations made by nationalist, liberal, and leftist opponents of the revolutionary government. Ahmad Khomeini, Ayatollah Khomeini's son, in a letter of April 29, 1989 to Montazeri, claimed that his father had hinted as early as 1983 that Montazeri was in "real danger of being influenced by the enemies of the Islamic Republic." Matters got worse in the summer of 1988, when Montazeri vehemently protested the mass execution of "members of the Baghdad-based Munafiqin," Mujahidin prisoners executed in revenge for an invasion of western Iran that the Mujahidin's National Liberation Army launched from Iraqi bases on July 26, 1988.

As of mid-year 1989, the Iranian constitution was under review, with plans to amend it in time for approval by a referendum in July 1989, when Iran's new president is also scheduled to be elected. On April 24, 1989, Khomeini issued an edict appointing a 20-member group (to be expanded to a 25-member committee after the selection of five additional members by the Majlis) with the responsibility of reviewing the constitution. This committee, known as "The Council of the Reappraisal of the Constitution of the Islamic Republic of Iran" (CRC) (*showra-ye baznegari-ye quanun-e asasi-ye Jomhuri-ye Eslami-ye Iran*), was chaired by Ayatollah Ali Meshkini. President Khamenei and Speaker Hashemi-Rafsanjani were elected as vice presidents of the CRC. The council's work was entrusted to four smaller committees dealing with the issue of leadership, the executive branch, the judiciary, and the media, or the "Voice and Vision."

The selection of Ayatollah Khamenei as the new Iranian spiritual leader and the election of Hashemi-Rafsanjani as president are likely to result in more pragmatic domestic and foreign policies. This change is bound to affect Iran's policy regarding America.

There is nothing, of course, to stop Americans from hoping for a democratic and pluralistic Iran, but any normalization of US relations with Iran must take into account the aspiration of Iranians to arrive at a consensus on the shape and form of a truly independent Islamic Iran. The fact that both Washington and Tehran have retained the option of eventually improving relations with each other can provide an opportunity during the second decade of the Iranian Revolution for open and constructive dialogue between the two nations based on mutual interest and respect.

NOTES

1. Warren Christopher (ed.), *American Hostages in Iran: The Conduct of a Crisis* (New Haven, CT: Yale University Press, 1985), p. 392.
2. These are rounded figures on awards. For the exact amounts see *Iranian*

Assets Litigation Reporter, November 11, 1988, p. 16541, published twice monthly by Andrews Publications, Inc., Edgemont, PA.

3. *Washington Post*, July 23, 1983.

4. Foreign Broadcast Information Service (FBIS), *Daily Reports—South Asia*, November 5, 1986, p. I-6.

5. See the *New York Times*, October 9, 1987. For reports on how concern over Soviet projection of power into the Gulf region led the Reagan administration to jump at the Kuwaiti request for protection of its tankers, see also *New York Times*, May 26, 1987.

6. For the text of Hashemi-Rafsanjani's May 5, 1989 sermon, see FBIS—*Near East and South Asia*, May 8, 1989, pp. 58-63.

7. *Ibid.*, February 24, 1989, pp. 58-66.

8. *Ibid.*, April 10, 1989, p. 54.

9. *Ibid.*, May 19, 1989, pp. 53-54.

10. For the text of Montazeri's letter of resignation and Khomeini's reply, see *ibid.*, March 29, 1989, pp. 38-39.

Contributors

Shaul Bakhash is Clarence Robinson Professor of History at George Mason University and author of *Reign of the Ayatollahs: Iran and the Islamic Revolution* (New York: Basic Books, 1984). He is currently a fellow at the Woodrow Wilson International Center for Scholars in Washington, DC.

Richard Cottam is University Professor, Department of Political Science, University of Pittsburgh. His latest book is *Iran and the United States: A Cold War Case Study* (Pittsburgh, PA: University of Pittsburgh Press, 1988).

Shireen Hunter is deputy director of the Middle East Studies Program at the Center for Strategic and International Studies, Washington, DC. She is the author of *Iran and the World: Continuity in a Revolutionary Decade* (Bloomington, IN: Indiana University Press, 1990).

Sir Anthony Parsons was British ambassador to Iran (1974-1979) and is the author of *The Pride and the Fall* (London: Jonathan Cape, 1984). This chapter also appears in *Iran: The Khomeini Revolution*, edited by Martin Wright (London: Longman, 1989).

R. K. Ramazani is Harry F. Byrd, Jr., Professor of Government and Foreign Affairs and director of the Gulf Cooperation Council Studies Project at the University of Virginia. He is the author of numerous articles and book chapters and ten books, including *Revolutionary Iran: Challenge and Response in the Middle East* (Baltimore, MD: Johns Hopkins University Press, 1986; paperback 1988).

Gary Sick is adjunct professor of Middle East politics and fellow at the Research Institute on International Change at Columbia University. He is the author of *All Fall Down: America's Tragic Encounter with Iran* (New York: Random House, 1985).

Index

Abu Musa, 109

Accommodators in Iran: characteristics of, 11-12; and Iraq, 18-19; members of, 15, 25n.22; opposition of, 18-19, 26n.26; voting by, 18

Adam-e amadegi ("unpreparedness"), 138

Afghanistan: and Iran, 89-90, 93, 94, 98-99, 102n.18; and USSR, 58, 77-78, 89-91, 98

Ahmad, Jalal Al-e, 65

Airbus incident, 118-19, 131-32

Akhundi, Muhammad Baqer, 35

Algiers agreement (1975), 105-6, 107-9

Amoli, Ayatollah Abdullah Javadi, 99

Anglican Church, in Iran, 74

Anglo-Iranian Oil Company, 72

Ansari, Muhammad Ali, 25n.10

Arabistan. *See* Khuzistan

Armilla Patrol, 80

Ashraf, Princess, 75

Assets of Iran, freezing of, 56-57, 126, 128

Audisi, Zuhayr Muhammad Said al-, 122n.9

Azarbayjan, 55

Aziz, Tariq, 107

Bahrain, 57

Bakhtiar, Shapour, 15, 75, 76

Baluchi, 13

Bani-Sadr, Abol Hasan: and assets, freezing of, 56-57, 126; and Beheshti, 56; defeat of, 22; "equidistance" policy of, 54; in exile, 73, 75, 76, 88; and France, 73, 76; and Hashemi-Rafsanjani, 56; and hostage crisis, 55, 56; and Khomeini, 8; and M. Montazeri, 56; and Raja'i, 56; and USSR, 87; strengths of, 17; and Western nations, 54, 67n.12

Basra, 123n.16

Bazargan, Mehdi: and Brzezinski, 53, 87, 130; cabinet of, 5; and centralization, 8; defeat of, 22, 87; as elite, 4; and extremists, 53; and Freedom Front, 6; and

Iran Liberation Front, 51, 65; as Kerensky of Iranian revolution, 6; and Khomeini, 5, 6, 7, 8-9, 50, 51; and M. Montazeri, 56; and *movazeneh-ye manfi*, 51, 52-53, 54, 86; and National Front, 6; popularity of, 17; as prime minister, 5; resignation of, 52, 54; and Soviet-Iranian treaty (1921), 52; and USSR, 86; and *tavazon*, 50, 53; and US, 50, 51; weaknesses of, 5-7; and Yazdi, 53

Beheshti, Muhammad, 56

Belgium, 80-81

Benyahia, Muhammad, 111, 122n.9

Bitarafi ("impartiality"), 50

Bovin, Alexander, 102n.10

Brezhnev, Leonid, 60

Bridgeton (ship), 131

Brinton, Crane, xii

Britain: and Central Treaty Organization, 72; and Iran, ix, 70, 71-72, 74-75, 77, 78, 82, 83, 84, 85, 91, 102n.25, 133, 134; and Iran-Iraq war, 80, 81; and Khomeini, 71; and Muhammad Reza Shah Pahlavi, 72; and Reza Shah Pahlavi, 72

British Embassy (Tehran), 74-75

Brown, Harold, 54, 67n.11

Brzezinski, Zbigniew, 53, 87, 130

Bush, George, 66, 133, 136

Canada, 61, 102n.25, 133

Caroline case, 107-8

Carter, Jimmy, 125, 126

CENTO, 51, 72, 86

Central Intelligence Agency (CIA), 126

Central Treaty Organization (CENTO), 51, 72, 86

Chernenko, Konstantin, 60-61

China, 93, 135

Chirac, Jacques, 76

Christopher, Warren, 126

CIA, 126

Constellation (ship), 54

Constitution of Iran, 55, 139-40

142

146

Index

land seizures, 34; and Mahmudi-Golpaygani, 38, 45, 47n.45; and Majlis, 27; and migrants, 34; and Movahedi-Kermani, 38; and Movahedi-Savuji, 37; purposes of, 31-32; and Shushtari, 32, 33-34, 38; support for, 35-38, 40-41; and Zali, 33; and *zarurat*, 34, 39, 40-41, 42. *See also* Temporary cultivation
Land seizures in Iran, 28-29, 34
Larak Island, 118
Larijani, Muhammad Javad, 98-99, 134
Lebanon: Druze in, 26n.30; hostages in, 57-58, 62, 83-84, 133; and Iran, 57-58, 62, 83-84, 133; and Iranian Revolutionary Guards Corps, 57; and M. Montazeri, 56; Shia in, 26n.30; Sunnis in, 26n.30
Leftists in Iran, 4; defeat of, 7; and factions, 16; and hostage crisis, 7; organization of, 4-5; and populists, 7; splits in, 7; suppression of, 16; weaknesses of, 7. *See also* Mujahidin; Tudeh Party
Lenin, V.I., 90
Liberals in Iran, 7
Liberation Movement, 25n.11

McFarlane, Robert C., 62, 114, 129
Magistrates' courts, 29
Mahallati, Muhammad Jaafar, 134
Mahmudi-Golpaygani, Abu Taleb, 38, 45, 47n.45
Majlis, 27, 40
Mazandaran, 31, 33
Meshkini, Ayatollah Ali, 139
Mirage F-1 aircraft, 80
Missile Technology Control Regime, 136
Moderates in Iran, 96, 97-98
Mohtashemi, Ali Akbar, 11, 21-22, 62
Montazeri, Ayatollah Hoseyn Ali: and freedom of expression, 9; and Khomeini, 138; messianism of, 61-62; and Munafiqin, 138; popularity of, 14; resignation of, 138
Montazeri, Muhammad, 56, 57, 61-62
Mossadegh, Muhammad: and Anglo-Iranian Oil Company, 72; and CIA, 126; defeat of, 49; and Freedom Front, 4; and *movazeneh-ye manfi*, 51; and National Front, 4; popularity of, 13; as secular nationalist, 19; and US, 71, 72
Mossadeq, Muhammad. *See* Mossadegh, Muhammad
Movahedi-Kermani, Muhammad Ali, 38
Movahedi-Savuji, Ali, 36, 37

Movazeneh-ye manfi ("negative equilibrium"): background of, 51; and Bazargan, 51, 52-53, 54, 86; and Mossadegh, 51; and Qotbzadeh, 54; and Sanjabi, 51
Muhammad Reza Shah Pahlavi: and Britain, 72; and Carter, 125, 126; and CENTO, 72; deposing of, 71; foreign policy of, 70; and France, 73; and Hussein, 105; and Kurds, 105-6; modernization by, 50; and Nixon, 49; and OPEC, 70; and Rastakhiz Party, 50; repressiveness of, 50, 66; and Shatt al-Arab, 105-6; and USSR, 52, 72; and US, 49, 51, 53, 66, 67n.3
Mujahidin: assassinations by, 7, 12; bombings by, 7, 12; execution of, ix, 138; in exile, 75; and France, 76; and Hussein, 15; and National Liberation Army, 76; opposition of, 7; and Rajavi, 17; strengths of, 17. *See also* Leftists in Iran
Murphy, Richard, 116, 117
Musavi, Mir Hoseyn: ideology of, 21-22; and Iran-Iraq war, 113; isolationism of, 61; as progressive, 11

Nasr oil platforms, 132
National Front: and Bazargan, 6; characteristics of, 51; as elite, 4-5; and Mossadegh, 4; and Sanjabi, 51
National Liberation Army, 76
National Resistance Council for Liberty and Independence, 75
Nixon, Richard, 49
Non-Aligned Movement, 111

Obeid, Sheik Abdul Karim, xi
OECD, 82
Olympics (1980), 87
OPEC, 70
"Open-door" foreign policy, 60, 61, 129
Operation Staunch, 116
Organization of Economic Co-Operation and Development (OECD), 82
Organization of Petroleum Exporting Countries (OPEC), 70
Oshnoviyeh, 120
Ovaisi, Ghulam Hoseyn-Ali, 75

Pahlavi. *See* Muhammad Reza Shah Pahlavi; Reza Shah Pahlavi
Palestine Liberation Organization (PLO), 86
Palme, Olof, 110